Oak Tree Controversy

Written by Susan Griffiths
Illustrated by Peter Townsend

Contents	Page
Chapter 1. *An angry town meeting*	4
Chapter 2. *On the side of the supermarket*	10
Chapter 3. *On the side of conservation*	18
Chapter 4. *A decision is made*	26
Verse	32

Oak Tree Controversy

With these characters . . .

Mr. Rajiv

Mrs. Ridge

Mayor Campbell

"Everyone

Setting the scene . . .

Ten historic oak trees which were planted by the first settlers of Oakville will be cut down if the new supermarket is to be built. The mayor of Oakville tries hard to keep control of an angry town meeting, where the fate of the oak trees will be decided in a debate. But people from both sides feel very strongly about the issue, and no one is interested in changing their minds. Everyone will hear the arguments for and against building the supermarket and then take a vote. But which side will win?

thought that they were right."

Chapter 1.

Mayor Campbell raised her heavy wooden hammer, and brought it down sharply on her bench. As she peered through her small glasses, the groups of angry people in the town hall fell silent. A difficult decision needed to be made at this meeting.

"It is now eight o'clock, so I call this meeting of the Oakville community council to order," she said in a firm voice. "During tonight's debate, we will hear the arguments for and against building a new supermarket in the center of our town."

The mayor looked around at all the people gathered in the town hall.

"There are people here who are for the new supermarket," she stated. "And there are people here who do not want the new supermarket built, because there are ten historic oak trees growing at the site. This is a difficult issue. We must follow some rules for our meeting, so that everyone has a chance to present their point of view."

Everyone in the town hall listened politely, but they didn't really care about what the opposing group thought. Everyone thought that he or she was right. Each group had researched their argument thoroughly and brought along objects to support their presentation.

A table on one side of the hall was covered in leaves, acorns, old photographs, and a small antique shovel.

On the other side of the hall was a shopping cart filled with groceries and a model of the new supermarket.

"First, each side will have a chance to present its argument," said Mayor Campbell. "As chairperson of the meeting, I will decide who can speak and when they can speak. Secondly, no one is allowed to interrupt a person who is speaking. Does everyone understand the rules?"

There was a murmur of agreement from the large crowd of residents. The mayor smiled, but she felt worried. Everyone felt strongly about the issue. What was she going to do if the meeting got out of control?

"Right, now let's get started," she said loudly. "First, we will hear from the people who want the new supermarket to be built. Who represents the supermarket owners?"

On the left-hand side of the town hall, in the front row, a tall man in a suit stood up.

"I do," said the man confidently.

The people on the right-hand side of the town hall whispered and grumbled and shuffled their feet. The people on the left side of the town hall sat up straight and ignored them.

"Please tell us your name and your title," asked the mayor.

"My name is Mr. Rajiv, and I will be the manager of the new supermarket," replied the man.

"Thank you," said the mayor. "Now, Mr. Rajiv, please tell us why we should agree to build the new supermarket where the old oak trees stand." She started to take notes.

Chapter 2.

Mr. Rajiv nodded politely to the mayor and turned to speak to the residents on the right side of the hall.

"Madam Mayor and residents of Oakville, I understand why some people are against the new supermarket. We want to build it on a block of land where there are ten historic oak trees. We will need to cut them down to build our supermarket, and that's a shame. But there are three main reasons why we should be allowed to build our supermarket."

Mr. Rajiv looked at his notes. He wanted to make sure that he gave an accurate explanation of his reasons. He hoped that the people on the right side of the hall would change their minds. But they frowned at Mr. Rajiv.

"Reason number one: our research shows that there are many people in our town who need a supermarket close-by. It's a long way to travel to the supermarket in the next town. Many older people can't get there. We will have products in our supermarket that you can't buy now in our town, and that will save people a lot of traveling time." Mr. Rajiv held up some groceries from the shopping cart. "Our prices will also be much lower than the prices of other shops in Oakville, so everybody will save money."

Half of the people in the town hall nodded and the other half frowned while shaking their heads. Mr. Rajiv continued.

"Reason number two is that we will be able to offer people many jobs to build and work in our supermarket. We can offer jobs to Oakville's builders, plumbers, electricians, and painters." He pointed to the model building and smiled proudly. "The new supermarket was designed by the best architect in the country. It cleverly combines modern design with elegant, old-style features!"

"Once our supermarket is built, there will be jobs for many other people in Oakville. Some jobs will be full-time, for people who want to work all day. Others will be for people, like parents, who want to work only while their children are at school. Finally, there will be jobs for older people who want to work part-time," explained Mr. Rajiv, counting the types of jobs on his fingers.

"Reason number three is that our modern, new supermarket will encourage more people to shop in the center of our town. By encouraging more people to come into the center of town, we'll make the other shops busier, too. The shopkeepers will have more customers, and they'll be able to offer more jobs for people, too." Mr. Rajiv held up his hands proudly to show how many types of jobs would be created.

At that moment, Mr. Rajiv was rudely interrupted.

"Who wants to come to a town center that has only concrete buildings and too much traffic?" asked a woman from the right side of the town hall. "I certainly don't!" she said, as she raised her arms, looking very upset. "What sort of town wants huge delivery trucks and shopping carts clogging up their streets? People want beautiful trees that have taken a hundred years to grow!"

The mayor banged her wooden hammer heavily on the bench, but the woman ignored her.

"My great-grandfather was one of the people who planted those oak trees!" exclaimed the woman angrily. She sat down, and the people on the right side of the hall clapped loudly.

"Order! Order!" shouted the mayor, banging her hammer again. "Your side will have its turn. Until then, you really must be quiet!" She waved at Mr. Rajiv to continue.

"In summary," continued Mr. Rajiv, "if we are allowed to build our supermarket, our town will lose historic old oak trees. But we will gain many benefits. We will have easier shopping, lower prices, more jobs, and busy shopkeepers. This stunning supermarket will put Oakville on the map! We think that these benefits are more important than keeping old oak trees," said Mr. Rajiv.

Mr. Rajiv sat down, and the people on the left side of the town hall clapped loudly. The other half folded their arms looking unimpressed. They did not agree with anything Mr. Rajiv had said. They waited impatiently for the mayor to finish writing her notes and to call on *their* speaker.

"Thank you, Mr. Rajiv," said the mayor. "Now we will hear from the side who want to save the historic old oak trees. Who represents the people against the supermarket?"

On the right side of the town hall, in the front row, the woman who had interrupted Mr. Rajiv stood up. The mayor frowned at the woman over her small glasses.

"I do," said the woman.

"Please state your name and your title," asked the mayor.

"My name is Mrs. Ridge, spokesperson for the Oakville conservation group," she replied.

"Very well," said the mayor. "Please tell us why your group is against building the new supermarket downtown."

Chapter 3.

Mrs. Ridge turned to speak to the residents in the town hall. The people on the left side of the town hall looked bored. They whispered amongst themselves and yawned.

The people on the right side were all listening carefully and nodding as Mrs. Ridge spoke.

"Our conservation group has three very important reasons for wanting to preserve our historic oak trees," said Mrs. Ridge boldly.

"The first reason is that they remind us of our ancestors. When our town was founded over a hundred years ago, the people who settled here faced many hardships. The land was not good for farming, and many of the crops failed. Many people became sick because they did not have clean water or enough nutritious food. As if that wasn't tough enough, a great fire swept through the town and destroyed many homes."

Mrs. Ridge pointed at the old photographs on the table.

"Despite these disasters, our ancestors, who came from many different countries and cultures, were determined to make a new life for themselves. Slowly, they learned how to farm the land. They discovered clean water trickling from a spring in the hills. They rebuilt their houses from stone instead of wood. They refused to give up."

"When the worst of those early years was over, they decided that it was important to have a memorial. This memorial would remind people in the future of how hard those early settlers had worked to turn this place into a town where people wanted to live."

Mrs. Ridge picked up an acorn. "Instead of building a stone or metal monument, they planted oak trees as a *living* memorial."

"They hoped that, in years to come, people would look at their trees, remember the settlers, and think about how lucky they were. That memorial is what the supermarket owners don't respect and want to cut down. If we lose the trees, we also lose part of our history and our heritage. That would be something we could never replace. It would be very disrespectful to Oakville's early settlers." Mrs. Ridge looked around the hall. Her supporters nodded in agreement.

"The second reason we want to save the trees is that our downtown has grown so much in the last hundred years that there are hardly any parks or trees left. We are already surrounded by too many tall buildings, stores, and houses. And *our* research shows that people want to preserve the trees that remain. They want places where they can rest and relax."

"The old oak trees provide a place where people can sit and children and pets can play safely. Under those wide, spreading branches, people can have picnics and enjoy some peace and quiet."

"If we lose our trees, we will have nothing but concrete and glass and metal surrounding us," continued Mrs. Ridge.

"The third reason is that the old oak trees provide homes to many animals, including birds, lizards, and insects, that will have nowhere else to live if the trees are cut down. We people must share our town with other living things. If there is nowhere for them to live, they will disappear."

"Excuse me! If I don't have a job, how will my family and I be able to live?" interrupted a woman angrily from the left side of the town hall. "I will certainly have no money for picnics!" There was a murmur of approval from the people surrounding her.

Once more, Mayor Campbell banged her hammer on the bench.

"Order!" she said, looking sternly at the woman. "I will not allow any more interruptions!"

The woman sat down grumpily, and the people on the left side of the town hall grumbled quietly and then fell silent. Mrs. Ridge continued.

"The old oak trees provide a safe environment for all sorts of living things that depend upon each other and the trees for their survival. It is important that we conserve some natural places for our animals and plants. Our lives will seem terribly empty if all we can see and hear are cars and trucks rather than small animals playing in the branches and birds singing in the tree-tops."

Mrs. Ridge sat down, and the people around her clapped loudly.

"Well done!" they said. Everyone on the right side of the hall believed that their reasons were far more important than anything that Mr. Rajiv had presented at the meeting.

The mayor banged her hammer once more and waited for the people in the town hall to become quiet again.

Chapter 4.

"During the debate, we heard arguments for and against the new supermarket. This really is a difficult issue," said the mayor firmly.

"Both sides presented very good arguments. Now," she said, looking around the town hall, "we will have a vote."

People who worked for the city council handed out voting forms. Two choices were listed: to preserve the oak trees, or to approve the supermarket. Everyone noted their choices on the form. The council workers collected the forms when everyone had finished voting.

Mayor Campbell stood up and strode into her office to supervise the vote tallying.

Everyone in the town hall stood up, too, and started talking noisily. The people who favored the supermarket thought that they had won. The people who favored saving the trees thought that *they* had won. For thirty minutes, arguments between people from both sides raged throughout the hall as people discussed what had been said during the debate.

Suddenly, everyone became silent as the door to the mayor's office swung open. Mayor Campbell strode toward her bench. Everyone in the town hall sat down again and waited anxiously for the results. Who had won the vote? What would happen? Would the trees be saved? Would the supermarket be built? Everyone held their breath as the mayor sat down and banged her hammer once more.

"I call this meeting to order again," she said. "The results of the voting are as follows." She put her glasses on and read the results. "The total votes for building the supermarket: 120."

The people on the left side of the town hall cheered. That sounded like enough votes to win!

"And the total votes for preserving the trees ..." The mayor looked up at the crowd. "120."

Everyone in the town hall groaned. It was a tie! The issue would have to be decided by the mayor.

The mayor continued. "Even though it was not easy, I have had to make the final decision myself."

Everyone fell silent and sat forward on the edge of their seats. Mr. Rajiv rubbed his chin nervously. Mrs. Ridge fiddled with her earring. Mayor Campbell picked up a piece of paper and read out her decision.

Half the people in the town hall smiled and cheered and clapped. The other half looked very upset, and grouched and grizzled loudly. But which half?

You decide.

"Order! Order!"

Oaks
Green, shady.
Rustling, living, growing.
Leaves, branches, windows, parking lots.
Bustling, waiting, shopping
Bright, new
Supermarket.

"A breath of fresh air..."

"Whenever Paul Harvey congratulates a seventy-five-year marriage, I usually wonder what made it last so long. Bill Coleman has answered this question. He uses fresh ideas and everyday examples that have worked to give help and hope for all of us who want to someday enter the 'Tournament of Roses.'"

Tim Robbins, Pastor
Calvary Bible Church

"I had fun reading this book. Bill Coleman's sense of humor and language of the marketplace are like a breath of fresh air. The extensive data base roots the book in reality. The specific suggestions for applying the findings of this book leave the reader with hope and new direction. The graphics provide an immediate grasp of the concepts. The author shines new light on tough, abrasive issues such as competitiveness, gender differences, and making time for the relationship.

"If you want to make a good marriage better, or restore a marriage that has seen better days, this is the book to read."

Paul Welter, Ed.D.
Counseling Psychologist and Author

"Excellent required reading for couples wanting to get married and those wishing they weren't!

"Bill's witty, conversational style combines with essential information to make this book a must for every pastor's pre-marital and marital counseling library."

Rev. Jerry E. Breese
Faith Community Church

"Most of us need a book like this one by Bill Coleman. The most important things in our marriage are: commitment (chapter 2), love for each other (chapter 4), mutual respect (chapter 7), and faith in God (chapter 10). They are all covered in this book."

Ray Deines
Married sixty years

WHAT MAKES A MARRIAGE LAST?

Secrets For A Lasting Romance

WILLIAM L. COLEMAN

Here's Life Publishers

First Printing, October 1990

Published by
HERE'S LIFE PUBLISHERS, INC.
P. O. Box 1576
San Bernardino, CA 92402-1576

© 1990, William L. Coleman
All rights reserved
Printed by Dickenson Press, Inc., Grand Rapids, Michigan

Library of Congress Cataloging-in-Publication Data
Coleman, William L.
    What makes a marriage last? : secrets for a lasting romance /
William L. Coleman.
    p.   cm.
    ISBN 0-89840-293-X
    1. Marriage—Religious aspects—Christianity. I. Title.
BV835.C615   1990
646.7'8—dc20   90-33882
                                                                   CIP

Scripture quotations are from *The Holy Bible: New International Version,* © 1973, 1978, 1984 by the International Bible Society. Used by permission of Zondervan Bible Publishers, Grand Rapids, Michigan.

Cover photography by Visual Impact
Cover design by Cornerstone Graphics

For More Information, Write:
L.I.F.E.—P.O. Box A399, Sydney South 2000, Australia
Campus Crusade for Christ of Canada—Box 300, Vancouver, B.C., V6C 2X3, Canada
Campus Crusade for Christ—Pearl Assurance House, 4 Temple Row, Birmingham, B2 5HG, England
Lay Institute for Evangelism—P.O. Box 8786, Auckland 3, New Zealand
Campus Crusade for Christ—P.O. Box 240, Raffles City Post Office, Singapore 9117
Great Commission Movement of Nigeria—P.O. Box 500, Jos, Plateau State Nigeria, West Africa
Campus Crusade for Christ International—Arrowhead Springs, San Bernardino, CA 92414, U.S.A.

*Dedicated to
Faith Community Church
Aurora, Nebraska*

*Marriage has many pains
but celibacy has no pleasures.*
— George Roy, 1804

CONTENTS

How We Found Out 9

1. They Work At It! 12
   Great marriages don't just "happen."

2. Commitment Is the Glue 20
   This "old-fashioned" value is the key to longevity.

3. They Play Together 29
   Is your marriage as fun as it could be?

4. They Love Their Partners 38
   We can't define it. We don't understand it. But love is why we're here.

5. Learning From Our Parents 46
   Couples that last know what quality traits to borrow from their parents' lives.

6. Loving Hearts Have Ears 53
   Effective communication requires two essential ingredients.

7. They Get Tons of Respect 62
   Respect for your spouse says, "I highly value you as a person."

8. A Growing Friendship 69
   Good friends make excellent spouses.

9. Works of Art Take Patience 76
   Can you imagine telling Michelangelo, "Hurry up and finish that ceiling painting"?

10. Their Faith in God 82
    A personal faith can cultivate the basic attitudes necessary for a loving relationship.

11. A Partner You Can Trust 88
    Trusting each other involves more than believing in sexual fidelity.

12. Marriage Is a Swap Meet 96
    Compromise is not a dirty word.

13. What Do We Argue About? 104
    Almost every argument falls into one of three categories.

14. The Six Myths of Divorce 114
    If you think marriage is rough, wait until you try divorce.

15. Because of the Children 121
    If we allow them, children can make wonderful contributions to our marital happiness.

16. The Calculated Marriage 128
    Have your expectations about marriage been met?

17. Let Bygones Be Bygones 133
    Happy is the couple who refuses to hold grudges.

18. Christian Support 140
    The church and its members provide married couples with resources found nowhere else.

19. Confusion in the Bedroom 145
    Perhaps if we really knew how God felt about sex, we'd be less hesitant to approach the subject.

20. Similar Interests 151
    What the two of you find interesting to do together is what counts.

21. An Understanding Heart 160
    Understanding represents an investment. It does not come pre-packaged. It cannot be microwaved.

Just a Reminder 167

How We Found Out

Someone once told us, "Our marriage has lasted this long because if I ever left my wife, she would find me and shoot me."

And just when we thought romance was dead . . .

Marriage is in a bind. I think we all recognize that fact. The present trend is to gut our marriages. Not only is half the population getting divorced but another 6 to 8 percent of couples are splitting without bothering to file the papers. Broken homes are not only the reality but also the fad.

Even though divorce is probably the worst pain we will face in life (with the possible exception of suicide), law offices and courts are packed with people who want out. Whatever the cost, whatever the consequence, their marriage is history.

But in the middle of chaos and marriage failure, there are millions of couples who not only make it work but who also enjoy sharing a nest.

Those millions of couples led us to this question: Why do so many marriages make it? What is the magic which holds so many partners together?

To find that out we started to ask couples to explain the secret ingredients that were presently working for them. We went to three sources:

1. We asked 1,000 people, "What makes a marriage last?"

2. We consulted surveys and studies in marriage journals, books and magazines to see what the professionals found out.
3. We checked the principles we discovered with the biblical principles and incorporated them into our guidelines.

The interviews we conducted were in no way scientific. Our method was uncluttered. We gave people cards and asked them to write down how long they had presently been married, whether they were male or female and then asked them to list three or four reasons why their marriages have lasted this long. We don't know how many were left-handed, how many chew tobacco or how many were Seventh Day Baptists. Most people kept their criminal records to themselves.

What we did find out was how those individuals saw their marriages as of that moment. We didn't want most of them to think it over for too long for fear they would begin to posture. If you begin to calculate, you might also start to worry about what you should put down rather than how you really feel.

We asked couples and individuals to fill out cards. We asked classes, clubs, groups and two congregations. A pastor interviewed his class for us and we sent out a mailing. People were extremely cooperative. There is no way to thank everyone who helped with this project, but we do realize how important friends have been.

Cards were collected from most states, a few from Canada and one from a couple vacationing in Belize.

Most of those who were interviewed were Christians. However, non-Christian groups gave us the same answers.

We have decided not to bore the reader with the exact statistics. Since the information is based on interviews, the numbers are only general.

But we will give the reader a few hints. The reasons most offered were narrowed down to a little over twenty and we turned those into chapters. Of those twenty there are four which were mentioned the most frequently. The big four are:

1. They love each other.
2. They have a faith in God.
3. They are committed.
4. They communicate.

Not that those four are enough. Other reasons contribute heavily to an enduring relationship. It's also possible to have a good marriage and be missing some.

But those interviewed said these were the big ones.

I am greatly indebted to those who responded. They taught me a tremendous amount about love and marriage. They had learned by watching others and by living it themselves. Hopefully many marriages will find added strength and spirit from reading this volume.

I extend special thanks to Bob Combs, Tim Robbins and Jerry Breese.

My wife, Pat, has done a fabulous job of research, typing and editing this volume. Her help is always at the heart of each project we do.

I also want to thank Les Stobbe and Dan Benson of Here's Life Publishers for their encouragement from the inception of the idea.

May your marriage vibrate with love, purpose and fulfillment.

Bill Coleman

1

Great marriages don't just "happen."

They Work At It!

*N*o one teaches us how to sleep. There is no class on how to grow fingernails. Few of us have read books on the mysterious art of breathing. So why does married life have to sound like such a chore?

We would like to think marriage just happens naturally. Trees bud in the spring; the sun rises each morning; tides rise and fall. Since love, marriage, children and cute little homes are good for us, we imagine they also should arrive in orderly fashion.

Expectations play a major role in determining how a marriage will go. Couples who do not expect to work at their relationship often have the roughest ride on the back roads of matrimony. They believe marriage should fit easily, like a hand sliding into a glove. When some of the fingers don't quite fit, the partners are immediately bewildered and alarmed.

Idealistic expectations make it harder to adjust when conflicts arrive (and they may show up on the honeymoon). Partners who knew they would have to handle problems are not stunned when the first differences become apparent.

The Cornell Medical Center asked hundreds of newlyweds about their infant marriages. The couples reported that they discovered marriage "a much greater adjustment and challenge than expected."

In our interviews, we found that the phrase "work at it" appeared more frequently on the cards of couples who had been married longer. Younger couples seldom mentioned it. Possibly those who had been married longer had caught on to the basic reality of getting along.

Every young couple needs a Dutch Uncle who will look them in the eyes and say, "You are going to love being married *if* you are willing to work at it."

After thirty-three years one couple said:

She: "We learned what things we *had* to change and then learned to live with the unchangeables."

He: "We worked out the difficulties instead of letting them break us up."

After thirty-seven years of marriage a couple wrote:

She: "We are able to work out problems."

He: "Our expectations of each other are more in line with reality."

A lady from Dayton, Ohio, married twenty-six years: "You work at it and learn through difficulties."

A male concluded after forty-five years of marriage: "We worked at making our relationship good for each other."

Marriage Requires Adjustment

Most engaged couples would probably quickly concede that marriage will demand change. Unfortunately we seem to miscalculate what kind of adjustment is required: (a) We believe most of the change will take place in our partner, not in us. (b) We are poorly prepared to make personal changes. (c) We never dreamed how severe some of those alterations might be.

"I never imagined we would have different bedtimes," Lyle was exasperated. "Never gave it a thought. She goes to bed past midnight and by then I'm fast asleep. Finally I told her she needed to come to bed earlier. Did she hit the ceiling!"

"Sure, I knew he liked to work on cars, but not every night. After the first two weeks of marriage I became a car widow," Rachel complained. "I said something to him about it and all he could say was, 'You knew I had three cars before you married me.' Sure, but I didn't know they were his children."

Partners who did not expect to make genuine sacrifices for the relationship begin looking for an exit. If they can't keep things the way they want them, they believe the relationship will not work.

Many of us anticipated only superficial changes. We were willing to move our supper time from 6:00 to 6:30 (after all, we are reasonable people). We agreed to give up the sports channel during mealtime, but we didn't think it meant missing Monday Night Football.

> **Adjustments can be personal, deep and painful.**

Couples who are struck cold by the need to adjust frequently separate during the first year or two. They cannot entertain the possibility of a long-term relationship which demands sacrifice.

People who work at their marriage show:

- flexibility
- sensitivity
- humility
- caring
- willingness to learn
- understanding of love
- spirituality

Those who refuse to work demonstrate:

- stubbornness
- self-centeredness
- callousness

- pride
- rigidity
- carnality
- unwillingness to learn
- impatience
- xenophobia
- short-sightedness

The Adjustment Triangle

The tricky part of working at marriage is to keep your relationship in proper balance. Each partner must give up a part of himself without losing all of his individuality. The ideal comes close to this:

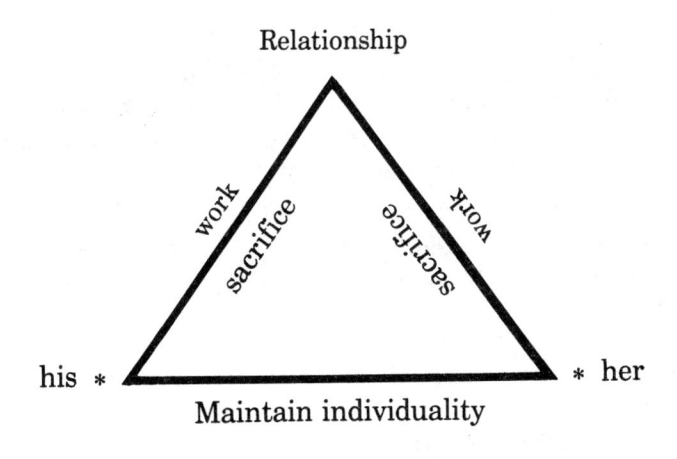

```
                 Relationship
                      /\
                     /  \
                work/    \work
                   /sacrifice\
                  /  sacrifice\
                 /_____\
          his *                * her
              Maintain individuality
```

If individuality becomes predominant, the relationship will suffer. Should the relationship become all consuming, the individual is lost. Caring couples tune their marriage to a fine balance.

When Pat and I were first married, we shared a medieval concept of marriage. Both of us believed the marriage should basically center in me. Nice work if you can get it. The only problem was that in order for that relationship to work, one person had to practically evaporate.

Pat's role was almost totally supportive. I seldom consulted her in the decision-making process. Most of the time I would call the shots knowing she would back me up. All I had to do was tell her what I had in mind. Our relationship looked more like a stick than a triangle.

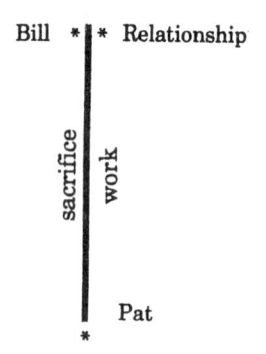

```
Bill  * | *  Relationship
        |
        | 
  sacrifice  work
        |
        |
        |  Pat
        *
```

Not that I recall browbeating Pat into this supportive role. She fully believed in "whither-thou-goest I will go" and all of that (which, interestingly enough, Ruth said to her mother-in-law not her husband).

But one day, by a miracle known only to God, Pat decided to become a person. My demure, obedient little wife went out and bought a mini-skirt. Life was never the same after that.

No longer content to take orders from her guru husband, Pat became part of the decision-making process. We had to talk things over. Make plans together. New sentences cropped into her conversation like:

"You go ahead. I have other things to do."

"Can you babysit Thursdays? I'm taking a class at the university."

"I want to get involved in a prison ministry."

"I need to go back east for a week."

And the amazingly crisp, "Forget it."

Fantastic! This meant I could have a second wife and still keep the first one, and not be arrested for bigamy.

This added a new dimension to our marriage. From now on we had to work harder at our relationship; consequently, we developed a better relationship. Pat's increased individuality made our marriage stronger, not weaker.

Now we have a working relationship in the best sense of the term.

Marriage Is Problem Solving

Several things marriage is not:
1. It is not problem-avoidance.
2. It is not problem-free.
3. It is not problem-centered.
4. It is not problem-controlled.

However, marriage is problem-afflicted.

This is exactly what the wedding vows mean. Do you remember saying something like "For richer, for poorer, in sickness and in health, 'till death do us part"? That means we agreed to work at it. And when we get tired of working at it, we will work at it some more.

When a problem arises, there is a systematic way to seek a solution. If a total solution is not possible, just the fact that you are working on it will itself provide promise.

Keep several steps in mind.

1. Agree to Talk

Take the guesswork out of your problem. We only increase the pain if we ignore the symptoms. Something seems wrong; take the initiative and suggest you set aside time to discuss it.

2. Identify the Area That Needs Work

Frequently we have two situations to deal with. Our partner may be pouting, shouting, boycotting, reacting, being destructive. We need to get past the obvious and work on the hidden. The goal is to identify why they are behaving that way. Isolate the problem the two of you need to work with.

3. Encourage Him to Explain Fully

Don't give easy answers or cut your partner off with quick solutions. Our need for someone to listen is enormous. Be an active listener, allowing your mate to say what he feels. While your partner talks he (1) may be discovering the real problem for the first time and (2) may find part of the answer as he speaks.

4. Discuss What Might Work

Two together will probably come up with a better solution than either one. Explore the possibilities together; show great respect for your partner's suggestions. We are not the Lone Ranger and seldom should we act unilaterally.

5. Agree on How You Will Work on This

Don't leave problems hanging. Your relationship is not a debate society which meets only to muse over theories. If at all possible, agree on what the first step of action will be and how each of you might contribute to this solution.

Occasionally, more time is needed before you take action, but you dare not simply stall. Discussions of problems must offer the prospect of being fruitful.

A young lady told me she was sick of it.

"I've heard that all my life. 'You need to work at marriage.' What happened to the playfulness?"

I told her to count herself fortunate. Many newlyweds have not been told about the work side. They enter marriage unprepared and fizzle out when the going gets tough.

Flexercise

1. What part of your marriage have you worked on successfully?

2. What part of your marriage would you like to work on?

3. Draw a relationship triangle like the one depicted in this chapter. How does your relationship differ from this? How is it similar?

4. How do you normally work on problems in your marriage?

This "old-fashioned" value is the key to longevity.

2

Commitment Is the Glue

When you complete a 1,000 piece puzzle, you are faced with a crucial decision. Do you want to add what it takes to preserve your work? If you cover the project with glue, it can be kept intact. If you withhold the glue, all sorts of dangers lie in wait.

Someone may bump into the table and jar the pieces loose. The cat might pounce on the puzzle, causing large sections to separate. Your cousin from Baltimore is likely to put his coffee cup on your prize and send the pieces sprawling.

By gluing the puzzle you make a commitment—you take the steps necessary to make the project last.

If marriage is the puzzle, commitment is the glue.

After experimenting with trial marriages, tentative relationships and short-term love affairs, we now recognize the critical ingredient to a long-lasting marriage is old-fashioned commitment. Surveys even among those who have been married less than ten years indicate that they have a serious hunger for commitment.

Previously some felt that a lack of commitment made marriage fresh and exciting. They imagined that couples who are not automatically committed tend to stay on their toes and resort to better behavior. On the contrary, many have become worn-out, always anxious that their attitude or performance may not be good enough to keep their partners around. Exhausted and frazzled, they long for a sense of belonging as basic as commitment.

The Marriage Dip

After a dozen years of marriage Dawn said, "Commitment to the pledge we made to each other gets us through the tough times."

Tough times grab every marriage by the scruff of the neck and shake us until we think we are about to fall apart. During those miserable trials smart couples hold on for dear life and just survive — and that is about all we can hope to accomplish.

Commitment is the key to longevity. Men who have made epic journeys across the sea solo knew they had to tie a line around their waist if they hoped to live through the storms. When waves filled the boat and winds rocked their craft, the rope held them aboard when nothing else would. Commitment is the line that ties us in.

Couples who fail to appreciate the value of rawboned commitment frequently split in the first three years. They are not prepared to weather the hard times.

A Big Dipper

Jana and Mike married with high expectations. They had heard the horror stories which some of their friends had faced and naturally they knew it could never happen to them.

For the first two years, their relationship did clip along with only a few hitches. They made adjustments and pouted a few times but generally rode the waves rather well. But by the end of the second year, Jana became pregnant.

At first they were excited about the potential of a new friend, but as the months passed their relationship sagged. Mike soon became aware that he had to share the spotlight with an unborn guest. In essence, he was kicked out of the playground.

After Meghan was born, Jana gave more time to the baby and Mike was allowed to drift out to sea. Without their realizing it, their relationship became cold and distant.

Fortunately they were able to sit down and define what was going on. They were in a severe marriage dip. Their relationship needed work, but it was far from the end of their marriage.

Dips come in all sizes. Some marriage dips last for a weekend, some for two weeks, a few for a couple of years. Every partner needs to know that dips are normal and temporary. Couples who fail to understand this frequently break up and head for the exits.

Smart couples tie a knot and hold on.

Smart couples lean heavily on their commitment.

Smart couples begin talking about ways to regain their footing.

Another Big Dipper

For many couples, another huge strain comes when their children become teenagers. Kids have a way of magnifying our natural conflicts and often produce new strains for us. Teens always produce new strains for us. Most couples will have trouble agreeing on the Big C's when it comes to teenagers.

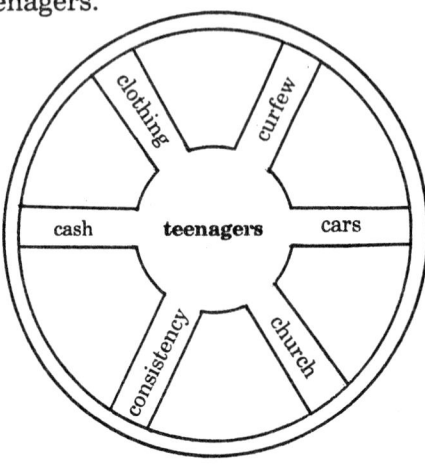

Even if our teenagers are angels, we are almost certain to knock heads over how to handle them. For people who have no underpinning of dedication, the agitation becomes too much.

This may help explain why the second largest divorce rate comes at the onset of the empty nest. Some couples have collected too many bruises from the teen-raising days to have any energy left to continue with their relationship.

When Connie and Ryan saw their girl, Kim, reach age thirteen, they were totally unprepared for the changes. Kim was far from getting into trouble, but she was straining to find her independence.

"Ryan and I were going crazy trying to figure her out," Connie explained. "One day she didn't want to come to meals; the next day she complained about the food. She was never like this before.

"Ryan and I would get into it over how we should react. He said leave her alone but I wanted to break her door down and get to the bottom of this. We worked hard to be cheerful around Kim so not to upset her. But when we were alone, Ryan and I fought constantly."

Committed couples remind themselves of several important facts:

1. Conflict during the teen years is normal.

2. There are many high points during these years.

3. This dip too will pass.

4. Couples who persevere have richer relationships.

Many marriages would probably be a lot happier if we knew it was all right to disagree over the children.

Accept Conflict as Normal

Our basic attitude toward conflict is a major factor in determining how long our marriage will last. Those who see conflict as a chance to grow not only endure but also see their love increase. Those who see disagreement as a series of mortal wounds are probably heading for the relationship's graveyard.

Difficult times have the potential of strengthening our marriage. Many couples have said, "After all we've been through, we aren't going to call it quits now." Broken bones are frequently stronger at the place where the healing has been completed.

If you buy that argument, conflict will pump up your energy and heighten your commitment. If each disagreement remains an open wound, eventually your relationship will bleed to death.

The problem intensifies when couples do not believe in the therapeutic value of confrontation. After a few arguments they move out and file. Consequently, they do not have time to gain from experience.

Enduring couples have taken the time to learn. They know that heated exchanges do not have to be terminal. Veteran couples can say, "Oh, we've been through worse than that and we got over it." Without commitment we do not survive long enough to accumulate wisdom.

How did Paul find contentment? He had *learned* it through experience (Philippians 4:11,12). Smart couples stay around long enough to gather some experience.

The Fear of Commitment

In recent years the concept of commitment has become a witch-like image. We picture it as an ugly creature flying about, making life miserable for married couples everywhere. There are several ways commitment has earned this reputation.

1. It Led to Abuse

Admittedly, many partners treated their spouses with contempt because they knew there was little recourse for a humble, dedicated wife or husband. Some came to hate the idea of commitment because they watched a parent suffer under this concept.

2. It Gave Way to Tentativeness

As the number of divorces increases, many of us think in terms of "maybe" or "wait and see" or "we'll see how it turns out" or "you never know what might happen." The prospect of commitment gave us claustrophobia. We felt smothered, confined and panicky.

Only now are some of us realizing the security of commitment and the terror of non-commitment.

3. Commitment Took the Place of Love

Too often we saw commitment as the ability to "grind away" long after a couple stopped loving each other. But commitment was never intended to be a substitute for love. Ideally, commitment is the bridge which allows us to continue if the road of love is temporarily flooded over. It holds us together while we bring love back to its healthy strength.

Nina explained how her marriage lasted when her husband of twenty-three years had an affair: "It was sheer, dogged determination. Sure, I wanted to shoot him, but I had made a promise about sickness, health, rich, poor and all that stuff and I wasn't going to let him go that easily. Fortunately, the Lord brought Ed back to his senses, but it was rough for a while."

Commitment is not a cage; it is a safety net. When the couple runs out of strength to hold on, the net is in place and prevents them from falling to the floor.

> **Commitment is not a cage; it is a safety net.**

A Sacred Promise

Most of the 1000 people we talked with saw their commitment as a pledge they made to God. Over and over we heard, "I promised her (or him) that I would stay together until death do us part." In essence they said that even when their partner behaved like a total jerk, they would keep the promise they had made to God and to that individual.

Not that there wasn't a limit to what they would put up with. Mary put it this way: "Number one, we stay together because we made a vow before God. Number two, if he ever physically or mentally abuses me, cancel number one."

She recognized there are evils to be dealt with, juggled and reconciled. Commitment does *not* mean any of us has to tolerate beatings of the brain or the body.

If I tell you I will drive your car and deliver it in San Jose, I have made a commitment and will keep my word. But suppose I accidentally crash off a bridge and sink into fifty feet of water. If I remained in the car because I promised to deliver it, you must conclude that I took my pledge to an absurd conclusion.

> **A sacred commitment does not say we are obligated to let our spouse beat us. That would be an absurd conclusion.**

Jesus Christ delineated the principle when He said: "So they are no longer two, but one. Therefore what God has joined together, let man not separate" (Matthew 19:6).

This supplies the framework for the sanctity of commitment. From here we work out our relationship with both compassion and tenacity.

When asked what makes marriage last, partners said:

"We don't believe in divorce."

"I made a commitment to God and my husband."

"Being committed to each other and to marriage."

"Willingness on both parts to stick to our commitment that we made *with* God."

"We made a commitment and believe in keeping it."

"God has joined us so we try to keep those vows."

Jason told me, "We flatly endured the first year. It was miserable for both of us. However, because we stayed committed, over the years we grew to appreciate each other. I don't know what I'd do without her now."

A woman who has been married for fourteen years said, "We have learned commitment as Christians and have depended on the Lord's leading in decision making. Believing the Lord brought us together makes our commitment absolute."

Resurgence of Commitment

The decline in commitment has understandably led to a hunger for its return. Calls for freedom, space and the right to do our own thing are beginning to give way to a longing for security.

Recently a survey discovered that among the eighteen to twenty-nine age group 37 percent believed it was too easy to obtain a divorce. They wanted it to become more difficult to break the marriage commitment. (Institute of Public Opinion Research of Florida International University)

We have seen what the breakdown in marriage has done to our parents, our friends, our own marriages and to children. A growing number are calling for an end to this painful madness.

Jim, a friend of mine from Ohio, wrote to say, "Actually, she would have divorced me a number of times had we considered that an option. Instead we both believe strongly in commitment and sticking to something until the end."

People dedicated to a relationship often have been treated like fools. But increasing numbers are now saying they are committed and they don't consider that dumb. Many of us are, in fact, proud of our commitment. And we don't mind telling people.

> Therefore everyone who hears these words of mine and puts them into practice is like a wise man who built his house on the rock. The rain came down, the streams rose, and the winds blew and beat against that house; yet it did not fall, because it had its foundation on the rock. But everyone who hears these words of mine and does not put

them into practice is like a foolish man who built his house on sand. The rain came down, the streams rose, and the winds blew and beat against that house, and it fell with a great crash (Matthew 7:24-27).

In the case of marriage, tentativeness is the sand and commitment is the rock.

Flexercise

1. What are the times when marriage is likely to take shorter dips of two days, two weeks or so?

2. If your marriage goes into the dumper, what is most likely to trigger a renewal of your friendship?

3. In your circle of friends, is commitment on the increase or decline? Why?

4. How would you describe your degree of commitment to your partner?

5. Why are you committed to your partner?

Is your marriage as fun as it could be?

3

They Play Together

Can you remember when the two of you were going together? Did you skate, bowl, play on a softball team, ride in paddle boats and splash each other, run to the ice cream store and practically fall down laughing? Well, many happily married couples still do that and more.

The dating world wasn't all light and lilting; you can recall the pain and conflict. But it was a mixture of ups and downs. Too often marriages have become so serious with few of the pleasant trimmings that accented our dating relationships.

Surveys indicate that a large number of satisfied couples manage to hang on to their playfulness. Make no mistake: Couples who play together have the same problems as those who do not play together. They often have oppressive bills to pay, a car which has trouble shifting into reverse, and a brother-in-law who is unemployed. They work hard, worry hard, even argue hard, but in spite of it all they are certain to make room for fun together.

"We still have a good time together," is a statement we frequently hear from couples of all ages. They have a mischievous twinkle in their eyes and would recommend marriage to practically everyone.

Childlike But Not Childish

In *Growing Young,* Ashley Montagu says the goal of life is to die young—as late as possible.[1] We are fortunate if we can find a mate who refuses to grow old even if his body starts to sag and bow. We are doubly fortunate if after years of marriage we can rescue a fossil-like partner and introduce him to the fountain of youth and new life.

What qualities of childlikeness are valuable? Montagu provides the following samples:[2]

curiosity	humor
imaginativeness	energy
willingness to experiment	perceptiveness to new ideas
open-mindedness	honesty
playfulness	eagerness to learn
flexibility	need to love

The extra good news is that these qualities can be cultivated and renewed. If you or your spouse has lost them, they can be regained.

I have a friend who is related to a fairly famous genius. His relative has more degrees than the equator and lectures worldwide. But if this "long-beard" gets near an amusement park, he turns into a fifth grader. There is no ride too scary for him; there is no food too sweet, no sausage dog too gaseous; there is no game which can escape his immediate attention.

His many years in the tombs of learning have not dulled his energy, curiosity or playfulness.

On the other hand, *childish* is a negative concept. In our society it suggests immaturity and a lack of responsibility. People who are insensitive and insulting are childish. They are adults who still do not come home for supper or don't change the oil or don't call in when they'll be late on the job. Partners who leave their clothes on the floor, tell you they hate your shoes, and stain your furniture show the marks of childishness.

Childish partners need watching and retraining. *Childlike* marriage partners are rare diamonds in need of protection and polishing.

Too many people married childlike partners and set out immediately to change them. They determined to erase their spontaneity, creativity and adventure. They were embarrassed by their husband's or wife's individuality. Those who badgered the childlike qualities into extinction may never know the special genie they foolishly forced back into the bottle.

If you have a childlike spouse, show him all the encouragement you can muster.

Playfulness Is Not Competitiveness

This is a familiar scene:

Bruce wants his wife, Norma, to play golf with him. Norma has never played golf and Bruce is a whiz. He finally talks her into venturing out on the course.

Immediately Bruce wants to accomplish two things. He wants to show Norma how well he can hit a ball. He also wants to see Norma become a reasonably good player within the next three weeks.

Bruce tells Norma how to hold her head, angle her left arm, wiggle her right foot and follow through. If she doesn't catch on quickly enough, Bruce becomes impatient and grumbles at her. Before long Norma gives up the game and vows never to chip a divot again.

Why didn't this work? Because while Bruce calls this playing, he doesn't really view golf that lightly. He sees it as competition. Norma must get good and get good now so we can compete. That's how Bruce knows he is having a good time. Therefore, he has no patience to allow Norma to come along at her own speed.

I wish our readers would send me a dollar for every couple that has given up a sport under conditions similar to those I have described. I could finish off my retirement plan.

Husbands or wives who must win tear the heart out of playfulness.

Caring couples want their partners to do well. They have no need to always win. Smart partners do not get angry when they lose at board games. Hopefully they love their spouse and want to see their mate have a good time.

Kerry wanted nothing more than to have his wife, Andrea, play board games on the living room floor during those cold winter nights. The only problem was that when Andrea beat Kerry at a game, Kerry became unglued. He threw fits of anger, accused her of cheating, turned sullen for the rest of the evening. Eventually he would play only the games which he was highly likely to win.

How did all of this make Andrea feel?

1. She tried to avoid board games.

2. When she did play, Andrea hoped desperately that Kerry would win.

3. She felt terrible about herself because she was forced to give in to a sick ritual of letting her husband seek his worth by moving plastic pieces around a board.

Who would have a need to beat his spouse at games? Lawyers, teachers, mechanics, doctors, construction workers, ministers and hairdressers. All of us can be afflicted by this destructive disease.

> **The person who must beat his husband or wife at games doesn't quite have all his ducks in a row.**

My wife, Pat, and I golf once a week and we have learned to forget the competitive side. One day she got a lower score than I did and I bragged about it to my friends. One person felt sorry for me and said, "You must feel terrible that your wife beat you at golf."

Just the opposite! I loved seeing the expression on Pat's face when she got such a good score. Her improvement at the game also meant she would golf with me more often. How can I lose when good things happen to my wife?

If competition is a problem, the immediate solution is to look for activities where winners and losers are not important. Hiking, biking, collecting, helping the underprivileged do not have to pit the skills of one against the other.

Leisure Time Is the Key

Some couples get along swimmingly until they have to face free time together. They seem happiest when their work dictates most of their activities and controls the majority of their hours. The prospect of time when they must decide what they would like to do as a couple is potentially maddening.

This may explain why so many couples seem to fall apart on the weekends. They have failed to get a handle on discretionary time. Frequently a husband and wife have a different concept of Saturday. (If they do not attend church regularly, they may have differing views on Sunday as well.) One partner sees Saturday as the big work day: clean gutters and shake rugs. The rub comes because the other partner sees Saturday as play day. He wants to go boating, watch a ball game, whip over to see the air show.

Because of their different backgrounds and set of priorities, they need to discuss what is valuable to each. Through understanding and compromise they can reach a mutual use of discretionary time.

Many couples have devised a shared-time approach. Saturday morning might be devoted to both partners working vigorously on the house, while the afternoons are dedicated to fun.

Then there are those who cannot agree on their use of time and end up doing nothing. One partner refuses to play, the other just as doggedly refuses to work. Eventually they dread free time because they are paralyzed by indecision.

Discussion and compromise could open this time up to the satisfaction of everyone.

On the brighter side, couples who tend to see their marriages as "fun" look forward to being together. They love having free time. They have discovered enough similar interests to guarantee that they will enjoy each other's company.

Inventory of Playfulness

Something to be alerted to: We could be spending a great deal of time together and still have a minimum of playfulness. We may be involved in activities which by their nature separate us rather than cause interaction.

The "Inventory of Playfulness" consists of three major questions (each having two parts) and will help you decide if you're making the most of your time together.

Question number one:

How often *this week* have you done things together which call for you to sit in rows and watch (e.g., watch television, attend movies, concerts, ballgames, etc.)?

        1   2   3   4   5

How often *this week* have you done things together which call for you to face each other and be active (e.g., cook out, play ball, sing together, paint a boat, etc.)?

        1   2   3   4   5

Question number two:

After spending time together, how often did you feel better about yourself, more secure and less tense?

        1   2   3   4   5

After spending time together, how often did you feel worse about yourself, less secure and uptight?

        1   2   3   4   5

Question number three:

How often in the past week have you laughed together?

1   2   3   4   5

How often in the past week have you felt a heavier burden after spending time together?

1   2   3   4   5

In determining your inventory of playfulness, the most important elements are trends. The trends over a period of time indicate where your relationship is heading.

Are you really together when you are together?
Does your participation tend to create good feelings?
Are your times marked by fun or pain?

Most trends are controllable if we recognize them and decide to make them constructive.

"A cheerful heart is good medicine,
but a crushed spirit dries up the bones"
(Proverbs 17:22).

"A happy heart makes the face cheerful,
but heartache crushes the spirit" (Proverbs 15:13).

"A cheerful look brings joy to the heart,
and good news gives health to the bones"
(Proverbs 15:30).

Is Our Humor Playful?

Humor is like sex. It can relieve tension and supply joyfulness; it can also cause pain and create deep-seated resentment. Smart couples study their humor and learn to apply it with an artist's touch.

"I always hated his humor," Alice said sternly. "It seemed personal and destructive. He thought he was the great put-down artist."

This is a common complaint. Too often we use *attack humor.* By making fun of a person, his job, his appearance or his value system, we think we will get a rise out of him and show how clever we are.

Frequently we resort to *relentless humor.* In this case, we kid about something and continue to ride that horse for weeks, months or years. Instead of developing a humorous atmosphere we make a deep wound and keep it bleeding.

Healthy humor demonstrates the following characteristics:

1. It is *mutually* funny.

2. It centers on *objects and events.*

3. It is at *our expense,* not our partner's.

4. It *indicates our acceptance of our partner,* not our rejection of him.

5. It *never* gets run into the ground by *repetition.*

6. It is *tasteful,* taking our partner's sensitivities into account.

Those guidelines deal with the joke or humorist. What should we say to the receiver of the joke? Mellow out! Humor is funny if we relax and enjoy it.

Playfulness Among Couples

When we look for a bottom line, this would be it. The test of compatibility does not rest in our ability to get along in a crowd, no matter how well we play volleyball together. The test is not how content we are when we are separated from each other. The crucial test is how well the two of us play when it is just the two of us. Those couples who play well as a couple indicate a great deal of satisfaction over a long period of time.

> "The two will become one flesh.
> So they are no longer two, but one"
> (Matthew 19:5,6).

Flexercise

1. How is your spouse childlike? Do you see this as helpful or harmful?

2. What do you play at well? What activities would you like to add to your playtime?

3. How would you describe your personality when you play board games?

4. How would you describe your spouse's personality when you play board games?

5. How does competitiveness affect your relationship?

6. What is healthy about the humor between the two of you? How would you improve it?

7. If the two of you could spend a day together this week, what would you choose to do?

---

1. Ashley Montagu, *Growing Young* (New York: McGraw-Hill Book Co., 1983), p. 6.
2. Montagu, p. 2.

We can't define it. We don't understand it.
But love is why we're here.

4

They Love Their Partners

*W*hy does a high forehead turn one person on and another off? Why does a person's smile look warm and gentle to one man but weak and silly to another? Why do you think a guy is so great that you couldn't live without him while your sister considers him a dipstick?

Love is the great mystery. We don't know precisely what it is and we aren't sure why it happens. But thank God it does.

We aren't the first people who can't explain why we love. For centuries great thinkers have thrown their hands up in despair. The author of Proverbs said he was totally baffled by four things: How an eagle makes a path in the sky, how a snake races through the rocks, how a ship finds its way on the high seas and the way of a man with a maiden (30:19).

Science may have brought us closer to understanding the first three, but how and why we choose to love someone becomes only more confusing as we investigate it. Love happens. If we are smart, we try to gain reasonable control. But most of us are a bit goofy when it comes to love. So be it.

We'll not strain ourselves trying to force a definition of love, but there are three things we can say with reasonable certainty about this phenomenon.

1. Love Is a Personal Experience

Most of us can testify that we are or have been in love. The experience is so nearly universal that we can accept the fact that it does, indeed, happen.

2. Love Has a Certain Behavior

While love is a feeling, it is also an action. The action part can be observed, checked out and certified. If we love someone, we act like we love him. It's that simple.

3. Love Is Highly Valued by Married Couples

The number one reason why marriages last, according to the people we asked, was because the partners love each other.

How Do I Know My Partner Loves Me?

The best way to observe love is to ask what love does and what it does not do. Just the fact that my mate has puffy glands is not enough reason to believe she loves me. *Love which is not demonstrated is suspect.*

Love cannot merely be a word. Love has a bitter sound if we hear it with our ears and never see it with our eyes.

"Every day he says it," Marie complained. "Brad is always saying he loves me but I don't really think he knows what the word means. He stays out late, doesn't call, almost never helps. Who needs his kind of love?"

Martha knows her husband loves her by what he does: "We love each other so much. Doug loves me unconditionally and is so supportive. He makes me feel very special."

George, married sixteen years, has seen the evidence of love: "My wife loved me where I was at. She could see inside me and see what I could become. She loved and encouraged me. She had patience and trusted in me in all situations."

Carole has both a warm and active concept of love after twelve years of marriage. Look at her entire answer:

1. I love my husband very much and could not imagine not being with him.
2. I believe in keeping commitments. I am committed to him and committed to doing my best to please him.
3. He treats me very special, always letting me know that he loves and cares for me.
4. We enjoy doing the same activities and share the same interests.
5. I believe that loving God and putting Him first helps keep my marriage strong.

These are not necessarily listed in order of importance.

Check out the key action words in Carole's answer:

being with him	keeps her commitments
doing my best	please him
very special	lets me know
cares for me	enjoy doing same activities
share same interests	

Carole's concept of love is not static. Love is not a condition like having the flu. She is not stuck with being in love. Love is not merely a wall plaque or a trite saying. Carole sees it as an ongoing, personal activity.

> **The Bible makes a strong statement concerning love: "Dear children, let us not love with words or tongue but with actions and in truth" (1 John 3:18).**

In *Counseling and the Search for Meaning,* Paul Welter says:

> Love is defined, of course, not by so many words but by the things we do and say to each other every day—and by the things we don't say and do.[1]

The love chapter of 1 Corinthians 13 does not *define* love but does *describe* love. How will we recognize love when we see it?

What love does	What love does not do
is patient	does not envy
is kind	does not boast
rejoices in the truth	is not proud
always protects	is not rude
always trusts	is not self-seeking
always hopes	is not easily angered
always perseveres	keeps no record of wrongs
never fails	does not delight in evil

> **If the F.B.I. investigated your marriage, would they find enough evidence to bring charges against you for loving your spouse?**

Love Is a Growing Experience

When a person says "I love Jan more today than ever," do we stop and wonder, *What kind of problems did he have with Jan in those early years?* Usually that is not the husband's intention at all. He probably loved Jan feverishly in their early years together and yet loves her even more today.

It is reasonable to believe that many "arranged" marriages work rather well. If the bride and groom accept the practice of their parents selecting a spouse for them and if both receive tremendous support from their families, they have a good prospect for a satisfying marriage. They can grow to love each other because they accept love under those conditions.

The Western world suffers from believing that love is something you either have or you don't. But love can be nurtured, developed and strengthened. Those of us who accept this concept of love can have an optimistic outlook under most marital situations.

John shared this insight: "Love is learned, not automatic. You have to be willing to love."

As we get to know someone, we have more reason to love him and not less. We may have married a person for a particular set of reasons. Over the months and years we collect more reasons to love that person. When that progression works correctly we may well expect to love our mate more as we grow together.

Love Grows From Intimacy

How do you feel when an entertainer on television closes his or her show by saying, "I love you all"? The performer means well but he or she has a limited view of love.

Love really counts when it comes from someone who knows us and interacts in our lives. Love cannot be painted with a broad, impersonal brush.

The love which a couple shares is based on knowledge of each other. If we get to know our partner and love what we find, we are creating intimate love. When we get to know each other better and find we love one another even better, we are developing a tight and lasting love.

This helps explain why divorce is so terribly painful. Often one partner realizes that his spouse got to know him well and did not love what he found. The agony is real because intimacy led to intimate rejection.

Intimacy is risky business. That's why many of us fight any chance for our partner to get to know us. We are afraid that to know us is to dislike us. Even after we get married, some of us work vigorously to keep the real self hidden.

Couples who want to love deeply need to accept this premise: *To know us is to love us.* The more we are willing to reveal ourselves, our dreams, our fears, our habits, the greater the possibility that we will reach a deep, growing love.

It makes sense that many couples who have been married for twenty-five years report that they are "more in love" than ever. Time has allowed them to become more intimate.

Knowing each other intimately takes three necessary ingredients.

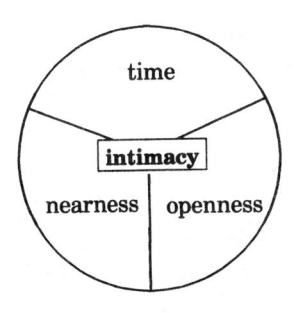

```
        time
   ┌──────────┐
   │ intimacy │
   └──────────┘
  nearness  openness
```

There are few shortcuts. Someone says, "You should get to know my brother. He could tell you a lot about me." But that wouldn't be intimacy. Another person declares, "All right, let's sit down and get it all out." That may tell us something about the person's impatience, but true intimacy cannot be announced, declared and completed.

Since intimacy takes time, it needs to be started as soon as possible. Too many couples are married ten years before they begin to dive beneath the superficial. They act and react on a surface level. They may love each other as fast as possible but deep-growing love is seriously restricted.

Early Intimacy and Beyond

Part of what makes love so exciting at first is the thrill of learning so many things about our partner. He has a neat sense of humor, he can recite old Beatles songs, he was president of his high school journalism club. With each unearthed treasure we find the person more interesting, more fun, more of a challenge. So many tantalizing revelations!

Unfortunately after the early revelations of intimacy, many of us hit a brick wall. We discover that we may be willing to open up to a certain extent but then we dig in our heels and resist more intimacy.

We need to make a conscious decision: *If I want him or her to love me more, I must allow that person to know me more.* In order to do that I must believe I am lovable. If I believe that to know me is to dislike me, I am unlikely to take the risk of intimacy. If I feel unlovable, intimacy is still possible but it is more likely to be a long, painful experience.

Once the early, tantalizing intimacy is over, the time has come to unlock the gate and allow our partner to see more of who we "really are."

If we are dedicated to the task of resisting intimacy, one of two things will happen. Either we will struggle through our marriage trying to guess what is going on (and many couples do this) or eventually we will tire of being married to a stranger and pack.

The alternatives to revealing ourselves are not good.

When we want to know our spouse better, there are two things we might try and neither one of them is nagging. First, give an example by revealing who you are. Take the risk and your spouse may follow suit. Second, be extremely accepting when your spouse opens up. Encouragement and understanding are the key. By these actions we create an atmosphere where intimacy is more apt to occur.

Love is many things. We are sure love is:

1. A feeling—And we do not pretend to understand it.

2. An action—We can best identify love by how it behaves. Love tries to involve itself with the person we love.

3. Intimacy—It's hard to love people we do not know. By getting to know them we grow in love.

4. Caring—Love is a deep passion which cares what happens to that person. We like potato chips; we love our spouse.

Isn't there more? For sure! These are simply a few areas where a couple can begin working out their love.

Check out what one woman wrote after two decades of marriage:

> 1. I love him enough to make it work.
> 2. He puts up with me.
> 3. He's a good lover.

Love is still real for a great many couples.

Flexercise

1. How does love affect the way you treat your partner?
2. How does love affect the way your partner treats you?
3. How has your love for each other grown?
4. Are you or your spouse more open to show your feelings?
5. What tends to hinder intimacy in your relationship?
6. What area of your love would you like to improve? Explain.

---

1. Paul Welter, *Counseling and the Search for Meaning* (Waco, TX: Word Publishing, 1987), p. 37.

Couples that last know what quality traits to borrow from their parents' lives.

5

Learning From Our Parents

One of the serious regrets I have is that I was not able to see a happy marriage up close. My parents divorced when I was fourteen and it was no shock. I cannot remember one day when they seemed to enjoy each other.

I'm not sure what I would have learned from my parents. But I think our early years of marriage would have been easier for my wife if I had seen a good example in my family of origin.

It's all right to have regrets. What's really important, though, is how I respond to the hand I was dealt.

From that marital desert I have been able to collect several rare jewels. I thank God for helping me unearth them.

First, I have a profound respect for the fragility of marriage. You do not kick marriage around or handle relationships roughly. They can be bruised, damaged and ultimately destroyed.

Second, when relationships are battered, they affect the people around them. Friends, relatives and children are frequently injured — sometimes for a lifetime.

Third, the children of divorce can go on to have healthy relationships within their own marriages. While statistics suggest that they have more trouble, they can also create very loving partnerships.

Fourth, we can learn a great deal from watching other positive marriages. While we may have been deprived of a good "in house" example, we do rub shoulders with many couples who show significant characteristics of love, caring, patience, faithfulness and fun.

The lessons we learn from a broken or dispirited home may be tough and often negative, but they are profitable nevertheless. As a result, I have an extremely optimistic view of marriage. It does work and function with a great deal of satisfaction. Having observed a dysfunctional marriage at close range need not warp my appreciation for this partnership.

Don't Blame Our Parents

It's one thing for me to acknowledge that my family of origin was discombobulated. But it's quite another to blame all my tomorrows on that part of my past. I am responsible to find out how I have been affected and then do something about it.

Too many of us become professional sufferers. If we are not careful, we learn to enjoy it. Read that again.

Look for telltale phrases, either spoken or unspoken:

"I can't help it. That's the way Dad treated Mom."

"Well, my mother just wasn't a very affectionate person."

"Mom and Dad never talked much."

"I guess I didn't have a great Christian home."

"My dad didn't take me anyplace."

"My mom never told my dad what to do, I can tell you that."

Statements like those may be true, but they become a problem when our past becomes an excuse for our protracted poor behavior. If my dad was a lousy talker, that is no reason for me to be one. Since I know how important communication is, I am obligated to improve mine.

There is a popular philosophy which blames all of our troubles on our parents. But we are not totally victims. Our past contributes to who we are but we are not obligated to let it control us.

> **When the bridge is out, we have a legitimate reason for not crossing that structure. But I cannot use that as an excuse for not getting to the other side. I must take the responsibility for getting where I need to be.**

Celebrate Our Parents

Even in a family which was disruptive, I can still pick out some strengths from which to draw. Most of us can pick out the good character traits which have been passed on. Take a few minutes and list five or six to help gain perspective. (Naturally, some will not be able to see anything to celebrate about their parents. If this is the case, you might seriously consider seeing a counselor.)

Ideally, we can be proud of the contributions our parents have made to our personalities. The Bible tells us: *"Parents are the pride of their children"* (Proverbs 17:6). We can help energize our marriages if we reach out and claim the gifts our parents have given us.

Let's prime the pump by suggesting a few of the strengths we might be looking for. You can add to the list to match your experience.

patience	listener
love	helping
availability	honesty
faith	cheerfulness
worker	dedication
giving	open-mindedness
financial	stability
forgiveness	closeness
energy	compassion
calmness	

This doesn't begin to exhaust the possibilities. Pick, choose and add as it fits your flavor. Your list may or may not have any of those I've suggested—they're not required. Your selections will be highly individualistic.

Hopefully this exercise opens the flow to all kinds of realizations. There is much for us to celebrate and emulate from our parents.

Some of us are, unfortunately, still shackled to a handful of bitter experiences from our adolescent years. By celebrating our parents' strengths we could begin the healing process from those turbulent times.

How, exactly, do we "celebrate"? By demonstrating that we are pleased. How do we demonstrate that we are pleased about the strengths our parents gave us? Do we prepare a stuffed pig? Do we sprinkle their patio with blueberries? Do we give them a year's supply of Polish sausage? As pleasant as these may sound, there are probably more appropriate ways to display our feelings. Let me suggest a couple.

Celebrate by Telling Our Parents

When we express our appreciation to our parents we reinforce, confirm, bond, release and all those other constructive actions. One of the greatest gifts we can give our parents is to tell them specifically how they have helped us. Both parent and child become fulfilled by this generous and honest exchange.

Celebrate by Exercising Those Positive Qualities

By now our rebellious years should be waning. For a long time many of us tried every way possible to be different from our parents. When we marry, we should begin a new maturity which allows us the luxury of copying our parents. We are sensible enough to say, "My mother was great at helping my dad. I'd like to do that, too," or "Dad used to bring Mom flowers; I ought to give it a shot."

> Freedom is a two-way street. Liberty says I do not have to copy my parents but it also means I am free to copy their actions when I want to.

Celebrate Our Freedom to Be Ourselves

The rebellious youth is busy reacting. He or she kicks against this, pushes that away. He has a hectic schedule trying to remember all the things he is not going to do.

People mature enough to marry have begun to *process*. They decide which character traits are reasonable, wholesome and kind. From that garden they pick behavior patterns which will serve them and their partners well.

Since we can choose our behavior patterns, we are responsible for how we feel and act. Thank God that we are responsible. That accountability makes us people.

I can choose:
> when to treat my wife kindly,
> how to treat my wife kindly.

I can decide:
> when to express love,
> how to express love.

I can weigh:
> what behavior is appropriate,
> which behavior should be avoided.

And how did I get to this freedom? My parents supplied me with the starter kit. I didn't throw their behavior away; rather I used it as a place to begin. We thank our parents for the starter kit.

Your spouse is different from the one your father or mother married. That's why we do not trace our parents' behavior. We take the liberty to map out how we will interact with the partner we love.

> **I'm not your mother.**

If we expect to use the identical behavior as our parents, we carry too many parental features into our marriage. Freedom keeps your wife from becoming your mother and your husband from becoming your father.

The Parent in Your Mirror

I still remember the day I looked in the mirror and said, "You look just like your dad." As a child I looked for that resemblance and even hoped I could find it. As a middle-aged adult I wasn't expecting that and was startled when I saw it.

Sooner or later you will see your mother or father in that mirror. It will be her eyebrows or his chin. You might notice the similarity in your posture or your handwriting. We aren't clones of our parents, but they are definitely there.

When he or she shows up in the mirror, we will be glad we took time to find the good traits. Then we will be able to say, "Sure, I look like him and I picked up some of his caring spirit, too." Or you will think to yourself, "I'm happy to look like her. She taught me what love was like." When you say that, you will celebrate the good qualities they gave you and you can be glad to be their child.

One of the most gratifying stages of parenting is to watch your children return home. You can remember when their major goal seemed to be to find an escape from your household. But after a while they want to return—for a weekend, a week, a summer, a year.

Parents aren't totally naive. They know a major part of that migration is caused by financial needs. But they also know that there is a longing for the emotional connection children left behind. They are beginning to accept the fact that there were some strengths at home which they have grown to appreciate.

When we asked why their marriages lasted, partners told us things like:

"Stable family upbringing."

"My mother's and father's devotion to each other."

"Parental examples—our parents have very stable marriages."

"Probably a lot of it has to do with my upbringing."

"My parents had a good relationship and my idea of marriage has always been good."

Flexercise

1. What good character traits have you picked up from your parents?
2. What character traits have you added on your own?
3. Have you told your parents which traits you are glad they gave you? When would be a good time to do that?
4. What traits would you like to pass on to your children?

Effective communication requires two essential ingredients.

6

Loving Hearts Have Ears

When Tim and Bev married, each knew how to communicate. Each had devised his own system of getting his messages across. The only problem was that Tim did not know how to receive Bev's communication and Bev had little idea of what Tim meant by what he said.

Bev believed the best way to say "I love you" was to show it. She knew words didn't mean much, so she busied herself with acts of love for the man she married. Cooking, mending and making things were her idea of communication at its best.

Unfortunately her efforts left Tim bewildered. Obviously she would do anything for him; no task was too much for this young bride from New England. But He couldn't figure out why Bev didn't say she loved him.

Tim was set up to receive verbal reassurances. Bev was sending task-centered messages by the hour and they were going right over Tim's head.

Not that Tim was any better. He came from a family of great kidders. If his parents liked you, they teased you every chance they got. They used teasing as an expression of affection. If they didn't kid you, they had reservations about you.

Night and day Tim teased Bev because he loved her tremendously. He believed you teased about the things you enjoy most. He kidded her about her hair because he liked it. Tim teased Bev about her body because he thought it was terrific. He made cute remarks about her dimples because they were knockouts.

And Bev thought Tim disliked everything about her. Her receiver said teasing was a put-down. Bev thought you teased about things you didn't like.

Neither person was unloving or inconsiderate. They adored each other like rain in July. But they were driving each other crazy.

> **There are two essential parts to effective communication: a sender and a receiver. Both have to function properly if we are going to get our message across.**

Find the Frequency

A radio program is sent out on a certain frequency. If I turn on my radio and can't hear the program, I have no right to complain and smack the radio. Because I am fairly sane, I am expected to turn the knobs until my set matches the frequency of the program. Only then do I receive a clear, understandable message.

Smart couples take the time to find the correct frequency.

Sad couples beat on the radio and exclaim, "There's no message on this dumb thing!"

Because we think communication should come naturally (as we mistakenly believe most of marriage should come naturally), we often lack the patience to learn each other's language. But couples who stay around long enough to pick up the right signals usually get to know a fascinating, caring person.

To accomplish this, I must be willing to work on two essential parts. I must make my *sender* as clear as possible and I must improve my *receiver* to the point where I can hear everything that is being said and not said.

1. What Is Your Sender Sending?

Love is not a word game. Lovers do not furnish a few clues and ask their partners to fill in the blanks. Hot lovers do not expect their mates to guess how they feel.

Caring couples supply all the evidence they can:

a. They say direct words like "I love you."

b. They add great body language like open arms, wide smiles, huge hugs and gentle touches.

c. They leave incriminating evidence like sitting by their spouse on the couch, fixing him a cup of tea, walking in the park together.

d. They give the gift of time to be available because they enjoy being in that person's presence.

e. They deliver surprises which say, "You are always on my mind."

The good sender uses verbal, visual, physical, emotional and spiritual skills. He or she is not content to use one avenue of communication. They work at sending messages in the most complete form possible.

2. What Is Your Receiver Receiving?

When a spaceship sends signals back from Neptune, the key to a successful transmission is exceptional receivers. They have to be sensitive enough to pick up even faint impulses.

Listening is a learned skill. That is always good news. It means that even the poorest listener among us can become better at receiving messages and understanding them.

All of us can become good receivers if we are willing to learn and practice receiving. Paul Tournier said many couples are engaged in a "dialogue of the deaf." We might be talking more and hearing less.

There are a number of practical ways to tune up our receiver and make it most effective. If we are sincere and really want to hear what our partner is saying, check the circle below. Each of the parts has a "turning screw." Which ones do you need to adjust in order to become a better receiver?

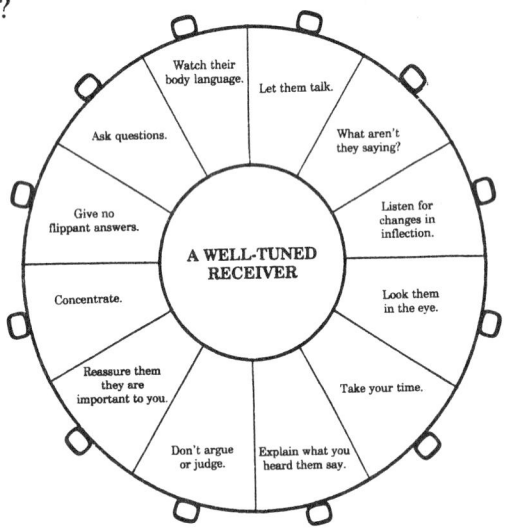

A WELL-TUNED RECEIVER

- Watch their body language.
- Let them talk.
- Ask questions.
- What aren't they saying?
- Give no flippant answers.
- Listen for changes in inflection.
- Concentrate.
- Look them in the eye.
- Reassure them they are important to you.
- Take your time.
- Don't argue or judge.
- Explain what you heard them say.

The Bible gives us three dependable guidelines about listening and packs them into one verse, James 1:19:

1. Be quick to listen. (Be a willing receiver.)

2. Be slow to speak. (Be quiet and hear him out.)

3. Be slow to anger. (Stay calm and don't jump to conclusions.)

Everyone who is married has a partner who is worth listening to. He is well worth the effort it takes to become a good, well-tuned receiver.

If you are married to a good receiver, hug him, kiss him, buy him low-calorie chocolates, take him to the honeymoon suite at the Big River Hotel, rent his favorite movie, give him breakfast in bed, massage his feet and generally love him to pieces.

Every Heart Should Have Ears

The ears on our head collect information, but the ears on our heart tune in for feelings. Some partners are great at assimilating the data but terrible at interpreting the passion behind the facts. (See the chapter, "An Understanding Heart.")

People who hear only with their head tend to say things like:

"I know, I know."

"Everybody has problems."

"We all need to grow up."

"Well, don't let it get you down."

"That's exactly what happened to Don; let me tell you."

Partners who hear with their hearts tend to reply:

"How did that make you feel?"

"That must have hurt."

"What would you like to do?"

"How can I help you?"

"I think I understand; is this what you mean?"

Christ told us there were people who "may be ever seeing but never perceiving, and ever hearing, but never understanding" (Mark 4:12).

Often we enter marriage with little experience in listening with our hearts. Our friends, our teachers, our parents and our ministers may have all dealt with us on a head level. *That dimension will not be adequate in a marriage relationship.* Ideally, we will keep our head level and add a heart level to make our interaction complete.

Do We Open Conversations or Shut Them Down?

Each of us has a set of keys. We can use those keys to lock doors or unlock them. Every day we put a key into communication with our spouse. If we turn it one way, communication shuts down; if we turn it the other way, communication has a high likelihood of opening up.

Some days the door is simply jammed. No amount of key rattling will get a wholesome conversation going. But most of the time you and I have a great deal to do with locking or unlocking that door.

Each of us possesses several types of keys or conversations. They may open doors or close them, depending on when and how they are used. We could benefit by developing an awareness of how we are talking. When we know what we are doing, we are more likely to make the best use of our conversation.

Small Talk

That's coffee shop conversation—a chitchat level where we say how we feel about last night's football game, the tax hike, higher skirts and the increase in school lunch prices.

This can be pleasant and even valuable as a social contact. Light conversation does the job of passing time and establishing friendship on a superficial plane.

Results: It allows us to crack open the door, but it is usually calculated to protect and hide our true feelings. It's little more than asking "How are you today?" and hoping you don't get an answer.

Philosophical Conversation

This conversationalist looks at life in the abstract. He explains how people in India feel about marriage or the current attitude toward tattoos in Madagascar. Like a water-skier, he can skip across the surface and cover a great deal of territory. Hard to pin down, he pretends to understand both sides of every issue and tends to tolerate most views.

Any attempt to uncover his personal feelings is only met by another side step.

Results: If this were the world of athletics, this conversation is designed to dodge more than it is to dive deeply. This type of talk allows us to keep the door locked but the transom above open so we can explain what we know. Low on disclosure.

Judgmental Talk

This is Mr. Answer Man or Ms. Answer Woman. While the other person is talking, this person is formulating a solution to the problem. He prides himself in knowing an answer to almost everything.

Normally this person is in a hurry for his spouse to finish talking so he can prescribe the correct medicine. He has little tolerance for discussion and despises ambiguity.

As someone has said, he has an easy answer for everything and it's almost always wrong.

Results: This type of conversationalist stifles and trivializes his spouse. Consequently the partner is not able to fully express her feelings and is deprived of the opportunity to help work out the problem.

Making Speeches

These types have learned to love the sound of their own voices. When we were children we used to shout, "Let me tell you about it; let me tell you about it!" No matter what the subject, we wanted to hear what we had to say about the topic.

This marriage partner is uncomfortable listening to anyone else and believes his or her views must be expressed. He or she knows a good conversation when he hears it—it was the one where he did all the talking.

Like throwing a bone to a dog to watch the animal chase it, toss any word or subject out and this person will wax into a considerable monologue.

Results: The speaker's door is wide open and a strong breeze is blowing out. You seldom need to ask this person's opinion. Merely raise a flag with a topic on it and sit back while the person talks. One huge problem is that while this verbal overachiever talks, he also puts his foot against his spouse's door so it cannot be opened.

Heart Talks

When someone sits down, looks you in the eye and asks what your dreams are, he is searching for your heart. And most likely he will find it.

If he listens intently, asks questions and shares some of his own dreams, the two of you have reached heart talk. The couple shares their hopes, fears, loves and doubts.

Only when both hearts have opened and made contact is this type of intimate conversation possible. Should either heart remain guarded or locked this level cannot be reached in a marriage.

Results: The couples who practice until they reach heart talk eventually have their doors wide open and share on a meaningful basis. Heart talk allows for the ultimate intimacy — which most of us want.

What Marriage Partners Said

Couples who have found the keys to good communication have discovered fresh strength in the relationship. Melvin had this happy experience: "The biggest single factor to help us grow back together was a forty hour weekend where we studied what God's Word said about communication in marriage."

After thirty-five years of marriage to Dick, Cindy said: "We've tried to keep talking about any little things that 'gripe' us."

Ken has been married to Loretta for thirty-one years and wrote: "We kept talking through the hard times and kept talking into all of the good times. Today we have a really strong marriage and know how to listen to each other and when."

Loretta agrees: "We really like to talk to each other."

Others have said their marriages have lasted because:

"We've taken advantage of videos and books to help us grow in the area of communication."

"We've learned how to communicate needs, love and desires (hugs, rubs and eye contact!)."

"We really try to listen and understand."

"We talk things out."

"We have open, honest communication in which we share dreams, desires and needs."

Loving hearts have ears and they hear what we mean as well as what we say.

Flexercise

1. Are you better at expressing yourself or at listening? Explain.

2. Look at the "Well-tuned Receiver" illustration. Which sections would you like to tune up?

3. Which of the five types of conversation are you most prone to use? Why?

4. Where and when do you and your spouse do your best "heart talk"?

Respect for your spouse says,
"I highly value you as a person."

7

They Get Tons of Respect

When Brenda became Mrs. Towson, she was excited at the prospect of becoming someone else. The wedding flowers, organ music and candles were a rite of passage to get lost in another person. The young bride ached for the day when her husband would become responsible for her life. He would make the major decisions, furnish the safety net and see to it that there was order in her world.

Even her good job was merely an appendix to his. If her husband's career called for a move, she was willing to abandon all and follow him to the far corners of wherever.

Brenda had picked up this concept from childhood. She believed the goal of marriage was to become lost in her husband. Everything would be his leadership, his career, his relaxation, his taste; and Brenda was looking forward to it. She was eager to become a non-person. It sounded like a relief to let someone else call the shots. She saw her role in life as a shadow. Brenda suffered from severe lack of self-respect.

It appeared as though this newlywed was happy. In a couple of years Brenda had her first child and soon went back to work part-time in a bank while her husband forged out his career as an accountant.

That routine would have continued for decades had her first child, Cindy, not been a girl. As Brenda watched

Cindy crawl across the floor and struggle to stand by the coffee table, a small voice spoke to the youthful mother. The message was simple. It said, "Girls are people, too."

That uncluttered message changed Brenda's life. The realization that women had wants, needs and desires of their own and had the potential for growth as human beings was enlightening. It gave her a new respect for herself.

Brenda's husband could tell the difference immediately. She let him know she would need him to babysit on Monday nights because she wanted to take a class. Soon they were planning vacations together, discussing their finances and sharing weekends.

No longer did $1 + 1 = 1$ (the one being her husband). From now on $1 + 1 = 2$ and their relationship gained a new perspective.

Not a "Revolution" at All

Brenda discovered a principle which is as old as the Bible itself. The Scriptures tell us: "Husbands, in the same way be considerate as you live with your wives, and treat them with respect as the weaker partner and as heirs with you of the gracious gift of life, so that nothing will hinder your prayers" (1 Peter 3:7).

What we've come to call the "women's revolution" is ingrained in the New Testament's principle of respect as a *normal* response of husbands for their wives.

Upper body strength and a monthly menstrual period are the only significant differences in the abilities of men and women. The Bible has always understood that. We are taught to *respect* that difference, not to belittle it.

In addition, the Bible tells wives to have an identical respect for their husbands: "However, each one of you must also love his wife as he loves himself, and the wife must respect her husband" (Ephesians 5:33).

One of the keys to a marriage that will last is *mutual respect*. Each person accepts the other as a full person. Any temptation to see our mate as less valuable than ourselves hurts the relationship and injures the marriage. The Bible understood that long before we tried to turn marriage into a science.

How many of us have said, "He (or she) treats me like a dog"? The English translation of that is "He doesn't consider my ideas, hopes, fears as worthwhile."

Most of us feel that way sometimes. Some of us feel that way often. A few of us feel that way all of the time.

Occasionally we meet someone who married a person precisely because he did not respect his partner. He was looking for a lackey who would feed his ego, be available at a moment's notice and warm his boots on cold winter mornings. Since people with normal self-esteem will not do that, he looked for a partner who had little self-respect. In effect he turned his wife into a servant and called her a mate.

A woman who wrote me (I will call her Roberta) was a victim of verbal and physical abuse. She remained with her husband because she believed she should be abused. We have foot scrapers where I live. If you work outside, you are encouraged to scrape your shoes before entering the house. Roberta believed God had called her to be her husband's boot scraper.

They were the perfect couple. He needed someone to knock around. She felt a need to be knocked around. His lack of respect and her lack of respect fed each other and resulted in a sick relationship.

What Is Respect?

The word *respect* has fallen into disrepair partly because of a false concept. Frequently we hear the phrase, "If you don't love him, you can at least respect him," as if respect is a low, grim, rock-bottom business. Actually respect is a high feeling, bestowed with honor and dignity.

Biblically, respect is akin to awesomeness or reverence and suggests, "I consider you, your life, your goals, your worth of such high regard that I treat you with honor."

We used to believe that type of respect was afforded only to men and especially to husbands. They were to be treated as kings in their castles. Smart couples now realize that she is a queen to be counted with equal deference and dignity. What she thinks, how she feels and what she dares to dream must be received with the same importance.

The choice is not either love *or* respect. In marriage the two are bookends. Love is dependent on respect. If we have little or no respect for our partner, we may be expressing pity rather than love. Once we have lost respect for the person, he is difficult to love.

Respect says this:

you are equal	you are unique
you are valuable	you are lovable
you are a gift of God	you are responsible
you are important	you are a person

Respect says you can:

have goals	have fears
make plans	believe
be heard	have doubts
be protected	exercise freedom
make decisions	make mistakes
take risks	fail
love	be angry
have dislikes	be ambitious
be curious	be creative
be disappointed	protest

and a great deal more

The Foundation Is Self-respect

Mutual respect is more likely to happen when a person has a healthy respect for himself. If we are self-defacing, we invite our partner to treat us the same way.

> **Respect begins with self-respect.**

Tanya was a perfect example. Whatever happened in her life, she seemed to put herself down. If her husband, Don, took her out to a restaurant, she never had a preference as to where they ate. When the family bought clothes, Tanya refused to buy any for herself. Anytime she played a game, Tanya tried to lose so everyone else would feel good about themselves.

Essentially Tanya treated herself as a non-person and she apparently relished the role. She accepted herself as one of life's trash baskets. Her message was "Dump on me. That's why I'm here." Naturally, if you are a trash basket you tend to attract trash. Since Tanya assumed that role, her family believed they were doing her a favor by going along with her wishes. Consequently, they tossed more and more trash into her basket.

The family occasionally protested, but to no avail. Tanya insisted that she be left home, wear frayed clothes and only watch television shows that others wanted to watch.

Why didn't her family grab her by the shoulders and say, "Hey, you've got to stand up for yourself"? Because it's hard to show respect for a person who refuses to respect himself.

Fortunately, Tanya woke up. She came to realize that she was busy making everyone else a person and neglecting her basic rights as a human being. And then this young mother told herself: "I don't like chicken wings. I've watched my last *Godzilla Eats Memphis* movie. I'm going to take some risks on my own."

How did her husband, Don, receive the change? He told me this: "I love her even more because she has decided to become a full person. She is more interesting and fun to be with. Now we plan things together. And I never respect Tanya more than when she says, 'Leave me out. I've got something going Wednesday night.' "

Too many of us confuse humility and respect. We often feel we can't have both. Actually we must have self-respect in order to exercise true humility.

Respect says, "I am a valuable person."

Humility says, "I am willing to sacrifice some of my rights for a time to help someone else."

If we say, "I am nothing. I can do nothing. I am worth nothing." then we have nothing to offer. Jesus Christ could exercise true humility because He was valuable (Philippians 2:5-7).

The Benefits of Mutual Respect

If we have total respect for our marriage partner, our relationship will be richer. The benefits are measured by the ton and not the spoonful. Let's look at a few assets to get our minds going.

1. Respect Releases Our Partner

When our spouse accepts the dignity of making decisions, we relax and let him run his own life. If we do not respect him, we are constantly trying to control him. Respect means I let go.

2. Respect Gives Our Partner Privacy

We don't need to know whom she talked with on the phone. We are not anxious about his mail or who she had lunch with. Respect says we do not have to crowd his life and keep track of every moment.

3. Respect Means We Don't Have the Answers

I do not know what is best for my wife, Pat. My role is to help her discover what she sees as best. When possible I aid, support, listen, even make suggestions, but I have too much respect for her to try to run her life.

A marriage partner who knows what his spouse should do demonstrates shallow respect.

4. Respect Is the Key to Companionship

We will never reach the goal of companionship unless we respect the person we love. As long as we think we are just *a tad* more important than our spouse, our love relationship will walk with a limp.

Flexercise

1. What are some things you especially respect about your marriage partner?

2. What are some areas you especially respect about yourself?

3. Is your self-respect on the increase or decrease?

4. Is your respect for your spouse on the increase or decrease?

5. Are you an equal companion in your marriage relationship? Explain how you know.

Good friends make excellent spouses.

8

A Growing Friendship

Before Irma Fay met Art she had built up a heavy load of resentment and distrust. Life had knocked her around more than a little and she tried hard to protect herself.

In the middle of all her pain, God managed to wiggle two miracles into Irma's life. First, she met a missionary trainee named Lillian Thiessen. After learning to relax with Lillian, Irma placed her faith in Jesus Christ.

Second, she agreed to marry this great guy named Art. For almost twenty-one years the two of them enjoyed life together until Art died of cancer.

I asked Irma what made marriage last for her and she wrote these five points.

1. The Lord put us together.
2. We loved each other.
3. We respected each other.
4. We were good friends.
5. Most of all, the Lord was the head of our home every day.

This is a love letter. You can read the openness, the positiveness, the joy, the genuine pleasure Irma felt because she had such a great friend.

Friendship may not be vital to a lasting marriage. Often couples are able to struggle their way to their fiftieth anniversary without particularly liking one another. But a large number of people feel friendship is essential to a healthy marriage. It seems crucial to a vibrant, growing relationship.

In marriage, liking and loving are not the same. We constantly meet people who are "madly" in love with someone they do not particularly like.

How often have we heard a person say, "I don't like what he does or the way he treats me. He's rude, domineering, self-centered and can be a real bear to get along with. But I can't help it. I love the guy."

What does that mean? Does she have a deep passion or sexual attraction which forces her to overlook the fact that he is clearly obnoxious? Is she so insecure that she would rather be with an inconsiderate person than be with no one at all?

We do not perceive love and like as the same thing. That explains why so many people are married to partners who are not necessarily their friends.

Fortunately, there are many forces at work in marriage. Often when friendship is lacking, other dynamics might hold us together. However, we ask a great deal if we expect a partnership to last without the key ingredient of friendship.

Internal and External Marriages

Marriages are held together by two forces. They are connected because of the needs and desires they feel inside and the needs and desires they feel from the outside.

Internal Marriages

A woman explained an internal relationship best when she said, "I really like the guy." Her feelings were simple, direct and uncluttered. Her husband rang her bell and she loved being around him.

Millions of couples feel this way. They want to go home, see their spouse and share themselves with that person. There is a strong "want" in their heart instead of

A Growing Friendship

just an "ought" or "should." A "want" marriage is the goal for good relationships.

Most of us had a "want" relationship when we were dating and when we were first married. The fortunate couples have managed to keep the "want."

External Marriages

Often couples are tied together because of outside pressure. They wrestle through their relationship with one eye on what is expected of them. Community and church pressure, parental influence, their children, prestige and stubbornness may contribute to their dogged determination to "stick it out."

External marriages run the risk of being overwhelmed by outside pressure. If their parents die or the children move out, the couple could lose the props which held them up.

Internal-External Marriages

Ideally a couple remains married for *both* reasons. They have a strong *want* because they like and love each other. At the same time they recognize the fact that they have assumed a certain responsibility. *Responsibility* is a good word. We do "owe" our children, our friends and our partner a great deal. Recognizing and keeping responsibilities is called maturity.

Growing Friendships

I can imagine someone throwing up her hands and saying, "Well, I guess that ends our marriage. Fred hasn't been my friend for five years; we hardly even talk to each other."

Don't head for divorce court that quickly. The good news is that it is possible for a couple to start at zero friendship and go to work and build a relationship. We meet couples who have accomplished exactly that.

Friendship does not happen by accident. It is usually planned, molded and nurtured.

Realizing that our props were moving out from under us, Pat and I began to work on our friendship. We added recreation, travel, work and spiritual ministry to our lives. We made sure they were things we could both enjoy or support. Through them we got to know each other better and rekindled our relationship.

Most friendships can't be stagnant. Most friendships do not thrive well on memories. Rather they thrive on such vitals as common interests, sharing, contact and helpfulness.

Marks of a Good Friend

I often ask the groups that I have spoken to or taught to tell me what they see as the marks of a good friend. In order of frequency, I've listed the qualities they gave me:

1. **Listener**—Society is starving for someone to listen.

2. **Honesty**—We don't want to be fed a line.

3. **Caring**—We want to know what happens to us matters.

4. **Loyalty**—We hunger for dependability and faithfulness even in the face of adversity.

5. **Spirituality**—Someone who appreciates more in life than the mundane.

6. **Time**—Availability. It is hard to be friends with someone who is too occupied.

7. **Laughter**—A need for someone to remind us about the lighter side of life.

8. **Sharing**—When our friend gives of himself and discloses himself, we feel free to do the same.

9. **Encouragement**—Someone to offset all of the put-downs we get.

10. **Common interests**—But no need to agree on everything.

11. **Unselfishness**—It's fun to be around giving people.
12. **Sensitive to your feelings**—They respect what we count as important.

We can begin with those guidelines, adjust them to fit our mix and "plan" to grow in friendship with our partners. It may take time and work but probably a lot less time and work than it would take to get a new spouse.

In the Song of Solomon the speaker says: "This is my lover, this my friend" (5:16).

Lover addresses the physical, the fun and excitement of flesh to flesh. Friend concerns itself with companionship in a broader, caring context. Fulfilled couples can have both.

Circles of Friends

In order to get a handle on friendship, let's draw three circles and ask where our spouse fits into the picture. For the sake of discussion we have divided friends into distant, casual and intimate.

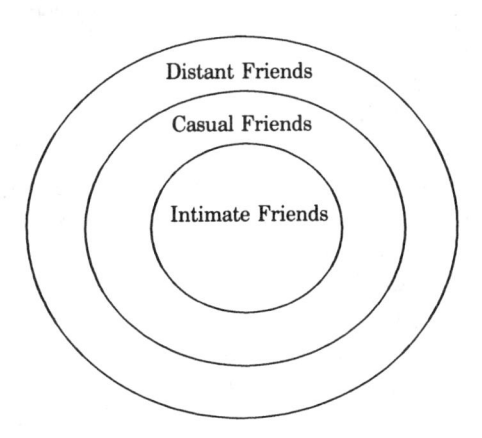

Distant Friends

Casual Friends

Intimate Friends

Distant friends are people we know on a cursory level. We meet them on the street or in the hall at work. We ask how the children are, who won the ball game, whether it's going to rain. Normally we don't talk for long.

Casual friends are the ones we sit down and have coffee with. Normally we express upbeat news or knock the government. We share our feelings on an outward level. Seldom do we describe details like fear, disappointments or dreams. If we start to share painful subjects, the person usually bails out.

Many of us have a spouse who fits into our casual friendship circle.

Intimate friends are the ones we care about the most. Generally we cannot relate to more than six to ten of these close companions. That number includes our immediate family. If we have too many intimate friends, we may have to push out family members.

These are the people with whom we take risks. We try out our dreams, explain our fears, possibly discuss our darker side, describe our joys, share our spiritual nature. If this person runs into difficulty, we will probably go to heroic efforts to help them. And they for us.

These categories are imperfect. Over a period of time some friends will drift from one circle to another. An intimate friend may become casual while a distant friend enters the casual circle.

Where does our spouse fit in this system of circles? The fact that we have sex and sleep together does not make us intimate friends. Intimacy speaks to how we relate, share and care. There are couples who have parented eight children without particularly caring for each other.

From week to week our spouse may move into and out of all three circles. One day he is intimate and the next he is casual. The question is where does he take up residence? Where does he live most of the time?

Unfortunately many of us are scared to death of intimacy, even with our spouse. Some of us have no one in the intimate circle.

How to Get Started

If we want our spouse to become our intimate friend, there is a starter kit which could get us rolling.

1. Tell Your Partner You Want Intimacy

Your spouse probably wants this, too, but was afraid you didn't.

2. Share a Slice of Yourself

Take a fear or a hope out of your heart and hand it to your partner. He or she needs a good example to follow.

3. Ask for a Piece of His Heart

Don't quiz him but let him know you would appreciate knowing more about how he feels and thinks about yesterday, today and tomorrow.

If we aim toward a growing friendship, we can establish a relationship that is worth keeping. Then we can say what Mary of Pennsylvania said: "I'd hate to lose my best friend."

Flexercise

1. What did you particularly like about your spouse *before* you married him or her?
2. What do you particularly like about that person today?
3. Which of the twelve marks of a good friend does your spouse display the most?
4. Which of the marks do you most often display to your mate?
5. What do you do or say to keep your spouse in the intimate circle?

Can you imagine telling Michelangelo, "Hurry up and finish that ceiling painting"?

9

Works of Art Take Patience

*L*otteries are tempting. They lure us with the idea that we can make a small investment, wait a short period of time and become instantly rich. In a matter of days we can have enough money to put us on easy street and let life roll from there.

A few people do buy the lucky number while millions of others believe they can. Instant success sounds appealing, but, unfortunately, it doesn't happen to many.

Marriage is not a lottery, a slot machine, a horse race or a publisher's clearing house. Good partnerships take time, cultivation and experience. If we are used to immediate gratification, that's hard for us to accept.

Dan, a dentist from Montana, said: "I wouldn't trade my wife for anyone else now — not after all we've been through. We understand each other. I'd hate to start training a new wife all over again."

Although his choice of words may not have been eloquent, we can sense what Dan is saying. It takes a while for people from different backgrounds to become comfortable with each other. Only with experience do we begin to appreciate the other person's timetable, their high points, their fears and dreams. A couple of months, even a couple of years, can't give us a rich feeling for how the other person ticks.

A good marriage is a work of art. Like clay, the relationship has been mixed, kneaded, watered, sometimes pounded, spun, molded, reshaped and heated. Patiently, the pottery has been worked into a form which finally becomes recognizable and enjoyable. Fortunately, the marriage was not thrown away during the early stages when it might have shown little hope of ever developing into a beautiful piece of art.

The Bible tells us: "Love is patient" (1 Corinthians 13:4). Love cannot flourish with fits and starts. Love cannot grow in a tentative atmosphere. Like new shoes, love must be worn enough for us to adjust to the fit.

When a couple says, "We've been married for more than twenty years and it just keeps getting better," they often mean exactly that. After two decades of marriage many couples have reached plateaus they are reluctant to step down from.

People who have a few fitful years (or months) and then decide to scuttle the ship never had the satisfaction of seeing a mature relationship. That's like eating green apples and concluding that apples must be bad for us.

Naturally, time does not heal everything. Just getting older does not of itself guarantee a better relationship. But patience does allow us the opportunity to mature, develop and find new facets about our lover which we might never have guessed.

Let's look at some hurtful reasons we lack patience.

Why Are We Impatient?

1. We Are Narcissistic

This is a two-dollar word which means we are in love with ourselves. It comes from a story in Greek mythology in which a young man falls in love with his own reflection.

When we are deeply in love with our own needs and desires, we have little time to wait for our mate. We want our partner to comply with our expectations and to conform immediately.

We see our partner's life only as it affects us.

2. We Need to Control Our Partner

If we allow our spouse to mature and grow at his own pace, he could suddenly gain some new interests which do not fit our pattern. He may take up Indian wrestling, bird watching or sword swallowing. Given too much time, he could want to become a whole person.

That would frighten some of us terribly.

Impatience says, "I know what you should become. Why don't you get with it?" Impatience is a lack of respect for our partner's growth process.

3. We Have Poor Diplomatic Skills

Randy wanted his wife to take up bowling. He loved the sport. Once a week he went to the bowling alley with the boys and enjoyed the sound of pins smacking, colliding and collapsing. Randy liked the laughter and the competition.

Understandably he wanted his wife, Pam, to join him on another night. Enthusiastically, Randy encouraged, pushed, persisted and eventually demanded that she give the sport a try.

You guessed it. Because Randy wanted Pam to play now, play well and play often, she gave up the sport in its infancy. Randy lacked the diplomatic skills to accomplish what he wanted so desperately. Frustrated, he resorted to pressure and lost the reward for both of them.

4. We Are More Comfortable With Anger

Since we have little faith in our ability to persuade and guide our partner, many of us resort to the method with which we are the most familiar. We try to intimidate him with our anger. Given the choice between patience and anger, we degenerate and use the latter.

"Whenever Carl was tired of waiting," Betty explained, "he would place his hands behind his head with his elbows sticking out. That allowed his biceps to show their full size. His eyes then went into that famous stare of his. Everyone in the family knew what that meant. The discussion was over and he thought it was time to get on with it."

Anger may be appropriate under certain circumstances, and certainly each member of the family has a right to display his in an acceptable form, but don't let anger smother patience.

The fruit of the Spirit (Galatians 5:22,23) provides a great many healthy, constructive emotions. Part of that fruit is patience. If we allow the Holy Spirit to control us, the more we are able to display loving behavior. The Spirit helps us reach above what we are naturally able to offer our partner.

Proverbs is packed with wisdom. A passage tells us: "Better a patient man than a warrior, a man who controls his temper than one who takes a city" (Proverbs 16:32).

If we choose the patient route to marriage, what are some of the benefits we are likely to reap? Let's sample a few:

Why Be Patient?

1. It Takes Time to Develop Good Skills

At first, most of us fumble through our marriage. There is some excitement over getting to know each other, but that isn't the same as the satisfaction of a mature relationship. After we get to know each other, we can communicate, anticipate and even predict on a far classier level.

"I've learned not to be so negative," Marge said. "Whenever we got into a discussion, I used to mention all the reasons things wouldn't work. My reservations would drive Peter up the wall. Now, if I want to get my point across, I try to be a little more positive."

"At first we were terrible in bed," Bob told me. "It's a wonder we lasted. But after a while we started to understand what each other needed and expected. We also found out what we were afraid of."

Couples can't do that over the weekend. Patience is the great teacher (if it has a good student).

2. We See the Person We Love Become More Beautiful

There are several types of beauty. One is young and new. Another is experienced and mature. Neither are more beautiful than the other, but the second type has a richness and depth that is incomparable.

Be patient and you may get to see the impetuous young husband become a steady, considerate person.

Be patient and watch a nervous, uncertain young wife grow into a confident woman.

Be patient and you could see an irresponsible husband come to realize how important his family is.

Be patient and you might help a speechless wife open up and show you what a great treasure she really is.

Patience is not a cure-all. Some people and situations will not improve. To the contrary, too many souls become more cantankerous and ornery with time.

But many of us know we are working with good material. The basics are there, but they may have not yet become what they could be. That person is worth the time it will take to see them develop.

Speaking of how Christians should treat each other, Paul wrote: "Be completely humble and gentle; be patient, bearing with one another in love" (Ephesians 4:2).

I want my wife to treat me patiently. When I mess up I expect her to know that I'm not perfect and please allow for my jerks, starts and sputterings. The problem is, though, that I am not always so generous in extending the same patience to her. Surely it is reasonable to treat my wife in the same manner as I would like to be treated.

That sounds like good marriage material.

Flexercise

1. What have you grown to appreciate about your marriage partner?

2. What does your partner do that upsets you? How might you handle it better?

3. What does your partner need the most patience about because he/she lives with you?

4. Do you see yourself as a patient or an impatient person? Explain.

5. As time goes by, are you becoming more patient or less? Explain.

A personal faith can cultivate the basic attitudes necessary for a loving relationship.

Their Faith in God

The number of people who said faith has played a considerable role in making their marriages last is overwhelming. In some way the "God-connection" has contributed heavily toward holding marriages and families together. Spirituality is alive and an important factor in the relationships of most of the people we interviewed.

This need not be too surprising. The great majority of people in the United States claim a belief in God. Nearly half the families pray before they eat a meal at home. As the communist countries open up, we discover that religion has not only survived seventy years of persecution but has, in many cases, thrived.

While church attendance may fluctuate, great numbers of people insist they are "born again," "spiritual," "believers," "Christians," or something similar. Faith is strong and healthy across our society.

Yet large numbers of "religious" people see their marriages crumble. Being "religious" does not guarantee marital bliss. There are too many other factors which make up the total package.

But no matter the variables, this fact stands: Most of the people responding to our interview saw God as a significant help in making their marriages last.

"We are both Christians. Our trust in the Lord results in trust with each other."

"I believe God brought us together and that He guides and blesses our marriage."

"We both know Jesus and try to live a life pleasing to Him. This ultimately results in a life pleasing to the people you chose to share with on earth."

"The Lord has been with us in our marriage and has blessed us abundantly. He has made a big difference in our marriage lasting, I'm sure."

"We're both born-again Christians who are committed to biblical morality which teaches you to resist temptation. This is not what you learn in today's standards of right and wrong."

Our interviews found that faith in God and love for each other were almost tied as the reasons mentioned most by those who responded.

Studies done by the University of Nebraska discovered the same emphasis. They asked people who thought they had strong families what they perceived as their most important family strengths. Respondents from twenty-five states listed these five characteristics most frequently:

- love
- religion
- respect
- communication
- individuality

During a seminar I asked the leaders of this study what they meant by "religious." They said it might have little to do with church attendance itself. Those families who treated each other with love, forgiveness, tolerance and patience explained they treated each other well because of their faith in God.

Faith in God seemed more subject and less abstract in the people who explained their marriages to me. Their faith was not merely ritualistic. Most spoke in personal terms and how it affected them which in turn caused them to affect others.

Many of the qualities expressed by happily married couples are similar to those described as the fruit of the Spirit: "But the fruit of the Spirit is love, joy, peace, patience, kindness, goodness, faithfulness, gentleness and self-control" (Galatians 5:22,23).

While these are spiritual strengths, they also translate into loving people skills. For some, these are qualities which they saw modeled by their parents, displayed by other couples or received fresh for themselves when they came into a relationship with Jesus Christ and the Holy Spirit. These couples place a low premium on negative feelings such as vengeance, anger, harshness, despair, indifference and meanness.

Often we waste too much energy looking for elaborate schemes on how to restore marriage relationships and we miss the obvious. Basic attitudes are at the foundation of loving families. The qualities which the Spirit supplies are the best ingredients partners can give each other. The more the Holy Spirit is able to control us, the more we are able to share these qualities.

Faith makes a difference when the faith influences our character, temperament, values, optimism and caring. If our faith is merely intellectual consent or a system of activities, that faith is less likely to have a positive effect on the way we treat our spouse and children.

Ideally, a personal faith in Jesus Christ gives us an increased appreciation for forgiveness, helpfulness, cheer, individual worth and other people qualities. The challenge to treat others as we would want to be treated is a basic people skill which is bound to strengthen the love in a marriage relationship.

Don't Use Faith as a Weapon

The Christian faith has received a bad name in some circles because too often partners have used it to abuse their spouses. Faith is ugly when it is used to gain advantage or to intimidate the person we reportedly love.

Bible Verse Beaters

Unable to persuade or compromise, the Bible verse beater will quote a verse of Scripture and demand change because "God said so." This approach is manipulative.

The Bible is used best when it guides us to the Spirit and we are personally changed.

Pray Others Into Submission

Have you ever prayed that God would alter your spouse to fit your expectations? Prayer is at its best when we invite God to help us create change in ourselves.

Lucky Charms

Faith does not work well as a love potion. Simple church attendance or the presence of a Bible on the coffee table has limited value. Only when we allow a personal faith to improve our treatment of people do we actually see faith making a significant difference.

The principle remains dependable: Our goal is not to change others; our hope is to change ourselves. Our other goal is to create an atmosphere where change in others might take place.

As one woman said after twenty-five years of marriage, "Don't try to change your spouse. That's God's job."

Faith Is Expanding

One man told me, "I grew up in a Christian home where everything was uptight. We tended to be negative and careful about anything we did. I'm really happy to be out of there."

Is our Christian faith a source which helps us expand or does it restrict us? How we answer that question may determine whether our faith contributes to a good relationship or hurts that relationship.

Restricting Faith

This type of faith creates a highly protective atmosphere where freedom, joy and expectation are discouraged. Rules are abundantly and heatedly enforced. There isn't much value placed in being a whole person or in self-expression. This shows a "bunker mentality" where everyone is defensive and fearful. This is not the kind of faith which is likely to give birth to a satisfying relationship.

Expanding Faith

This kind of faith in God encourages a couple to open up and be all they can be. Each partner has permission to spread his wings and try new things. They are saying, "Look what faith is doing in our lives." The restrictive group is more likely to say, "Look what faith is saving us from."

After eleven years of marriage, a woman said, "We made a commitment to God and to each other. And it's been fun!"

A man married twenty-five years wrote, "We both know Jesus as Savior and walk with Him."

The Significant Other

When our relationship hits the skids and we wonder if it can ever live again, we like to know there is an additional source which could come through for us. We like to believe there is a God who is working in ways we cannot see and might never understand.

We choose to believe there is a spiritual world and a spiritual reality which causes miracles. We like to believe there is a spiritual value to life which gives it an extra meaning and purpose. We want to believe we are not alone.

With all of this going on "behind the scenes," we can expect God to supply some added strength or wisdom to rekindle the love we have for our spouse.

This may explain why an overwhelming number of us believe in angels. Angels are not a medieval concept of

Their Faith in God

ghosts darting around wearing wings. Rather, we choose to believe that there are helping agents which we cannot see but are busy trying to bring good into our lives and relationships. "Are not all angels ministering spirits sent to serve those who will inherit salvation?" (Hebrews 1:14)

We believe in the supernatural and particularly in God. Our God is not limited to being a great therapist in the sky who busies Himself adjusting our personalities, though He does have a role in changing us.

Our God helps in "mysterious" ways, many of which we cannot identify or explain. The supernatural and the instructional influence God brings to our lives is able to have a great effect on our marriage relationships.

Flexercise

1. How does your faith affect your marriage?

2. Which of your characteristics would you attribute to your faith in God?

3. Which characteristics would you want God to help you improve?

4. How does your faith help you "expand" your relationship?

5. When have you felt confident that God was working supernaturally in the background of your life?

6. Is your relationship presently leaning toward:
    a. forgiveness, love, joy, peace?
    b. anger, impatience, vengeance, fear?
   Explain.

Trusting each other involves more than
believing in sexual fidelity.

11

A Partner You Can Trust

*A*t its best, marriage is a safe place. It's a harbor, it's first base, it's a shelter, it's your front porch when the town bully is walking through the neighborhood. Marriage means you can relax and trust each other.

I didn't begin to understand that until I met Larry. Larry didn't like to go home. He worked hard in the auto factory. When his shift was over, Larry stopped for coffee after work and remained at the restaurant for an hour or two. Each evening his social calendar was filled with bowling, committee meetings, sports events or whatever could pass as a reasonable diversion without making him look like a total derelict.

Larry had a wife and children at home, but he didn't feel like he had a harbor. His wife, Sherri, nagged, complained and believed she could spur him to greater goals by ridicule and constant demands. In turn he felt he could never let down his guard at home. Larry had dreams, hopes and fears but was afraid to share them with Sherri because he knew she would attack any trace of self-expression.

Every day Larry faced the dragons that roamed the world. However, the greatest dragon was the one waiting inside his castle.

This is how many husbands and wives feel when they cannot trust their partners.

A Partner You Can Trust

Ruby was just the opposite. When she had a new idea or was excited about a new discovery, she bounded home to share it with the person she loved. Ruby knew her husband, Gary, would give her a great audience. Most of the time he tried to supply air for her trial balloon.

Gary created an atmosphere where Ruby was free to be herself and able to stretch further.

Strong marriages are safe places most of the time. If they aren't, we learn to hate them.

> **Each of us has a burning yearning for someone we can count on. That's the need for trust.**

The writer of Proverbs expressed it this way: "What a man desires is unfailing love" (19:22). We are not looking for someone who rants and raves over us one day and tears us apart tomorrow.

Probably all of us feel let down and possibly betrayed occasionally. But the higher the degree of trust, the greater the chance we will maintain a happy relationship.

The groups and individuals I discussed marriage with gave me a great deal of insight into trust. At first I thought they were discussing sexual fidelity; however, for most people that was only a small part of trust. They were far more concerned about having someone to lean on and being confident that their leaning post would not fall down.

Trust Means You Can Take Risks

Have you ever had a friend with whom you could not take risks? You were afraid to bring up new ideas for fear he or she would say something like, "That's a stupid idea. Where did you ever come up with that?" He was still your friend, but you felt shackled because you had to carefully measure which subjects you brought up.

As bad as that feeling is, the pain is multiplied if the shut-down artist is your husband or wife. Like a stifled child you are reluctant to share your hopes and ambitions.

Strong marriage partners love to hear dreams. They not only listen well but whenever possible suggest ways to help bring those shadows into reality.

The loving partner will hopefully:

1. Be an active listener.

2. Try to understand the outline of the dream.

3. Make encouraging responses — if at all possible.

4. Ask to be kept informed about its progress.

Risk-taking also means we are not afraid to say that something has upset us. Expressed tactfully we expect to get a civil hearing to an honest attempt to improve a situation.

If we say we do not enjoy string beans, we don't expect the response to be an aboriginal war dance. We can take a chance on disagreeing with something that is going on between us. This means we have a relaxed, trusting relationship.

Trust Invites Our Transparency

In the safe haven of our relationship we are free to show who we really are. She can unveil both the little girl and the woman knowing that he will accept and love both. He in turn is at liberty to reveal his strengths along with his weaknesses and be assured that she will say that each are welcome as part of the total package.

"I had trouble letting her know that I enjoyed country music," Bob explained. "I know it sounds corny. I tried to develop a taste for classical, and when we were together I always tuned in classical on the radio. I didn't want her to find out what I was really like.

"After pretending for a year, I finally told her what my preference was. Judy was not only understanding but even went out of her way to listen to it with me. Every once in a while we go to a country concert and she goes along with a smile.

"I still play classical on the radio, and we are growing to appreciate each other's tastes. But at first I was afraid Judy would think I was deranged."

There is a reason she is afraid of dark rooms.
There is a reason he neglects the car.
There is a reason she is afraid to fail.
There is a reason he has to win.
There is a reason she dislikes vacations.
There is a reason he doesn't discuss his feelings.

Hopefully he or she will come to trust his mate enough that they can discuss those issues. Most of us would really like to show and tell our partner who we actually are.

We need to know we have found unfailing love. And even then it may be hard to open up.

> **Love is not totally functional until it trusts the other person (1 Corinthians 13:7).**

Trust Sets Our Partner Free

Do you know a married person who has a leash on his partner's collar and he considers that leash an act of love? He believes you keep your mate in tow as evidence that you really care.

When, and if, their love reaches maturity he will remove the leash and set her free.

Mature love does not necessarily take time. Some partners have a wholesome concept of love from the beginning. Others cut the 50th anniversary cake still afraid of losing control. Mature love accepts its partner as a full, free person and can be done from day one.

When someone in a B movie says, "I love you so much I'd rather shoot you than see you with someone else," you know he flunked "Love 101" and has no idea what he's talking about.

The reluctance to set our partner free to live out his own expressions says tons about the person who demands control. It shows how little he trusts himself. If he sets his partner free, his partner will act, fail, succeed and otherwise create movement. The jailer in the relationship is afraid he will not know how to react to his partner's act of freedom. Therefore, he aims to keep the person tethered to protect himself.

Wholesome relationships offer the freedom of movement. Anemic relationships pen up, tie down and seriously restrict the partner.

I asked Randy where his wife, Dee, was. He was watching their two pre-schoolers as they romped around the camp.

"Oh, she went white water rafting," he answered in a matter-of-fact tone.

That was the kind of relationship they had, so I wasn't startled. They were both free spirits who encouraged each other to try their wings. Non-traditionalists, each had the liberty to savor the adventures of life and yet they maintained their reasonable share of responsibilities.

> **Freedom is a gift which the Holy Spirit hands out generously—and it scares some people to death (2 Corinthians 3:17).**

Trust encourages our partner to seek his own identity and does not demand that he be totally immersed in the relationship. Marriage says that the relationship is more important then the goals of either partner. However, lasting relationships do not annihilate the value of the individual. Run that sentence by again.

Trust Tries to Understand

My wife does not always understand how I feel or what I am going through but one thing I can count on: She will try. Most of the time she will sympathize and attempt to empathize.

This means a wise partner will not fluff off my problem; at least, not most of the time.

The ideal is empathy. This means you feel terrible about being fired from your job and your partner understands because he or she was once fired himself. It's hard to beat this kind of relationship.

Almost as good is the ability to sympathize. This means your partner has never had an alcoholic parent but he or she will try to understand when you explain your feelings. We can't ask more than that if that is all our partner has.

There are some times when our partner is tired, wrapped up in his own problems or simply inconsiderate at the moment. *No partner can be expected to respond gracefully all of the time.*

What does this have to do with trust?

Trust means our partner will try to respond in an understanding manner—most of the time. We need to be able to count on that fact.

If our partner refuses to try most of the time, we will either find someone else to share with or share with no one. When we feel that our partner has set up a roadblock to stop us from sharing, our relationship is seriously flawed.

Carol married a great guy whose mother was an alcoholic. Because of his past, Don has some serious baggage. He had a limited view of women, didn't like to talk about his feelings and often had trouble believing Carol loved him.

Because Carol had such a different family, she could not begin to comprehend what went on inside Don. Often Don's actions and reactions seemed unreasonable and even disconnected to reality.

After several years of marriage and considerable pain, Carol dedicated herself to a serious attempt at understanding her husband. She read articles about what adult children of alcoholics go through. Timidly Carol searched out an acquaintance who had a similar background as Don and asked for help. Slowly she eased more information from Don himself.

Carol could not feel what Don felt. She never would. But she could come closer to understanding what Don went through, and Carol decided to go for that.

Don can trust Carol because:

1. She does not shrug off his problems.

2. She cares enough to try and understand.

3. She will accept what she cannot understand.

The desire to understand the person we love keeps us from getting disjointed and frustrated.

> "A man of knowledge uses words with restraint,
> and a man of understanding is even-tempered"
> (Proverbs 17:27).

Trust Is Free From Slander

Every partner needs the security of knowing that his or her spouse will bring any complaint to him and not announce it to the rest of the world. If you have ever heard a husband blasting his wife to his buddies, you know exactly what I'm talking about.

That doesn't mean we cannot kid about our mate. But even this has to be guarded. If your husband believes you handle money poorly, he needs to discuss that with you and not with his friends at the truck stop. When we discover that our spouse has done that, our trust factor drops like a rock.

> **Any attempt to hurt my spouse by slandering her in front of my friends is a betrayal of our trust.**

This doesn't mean I cannot seek legitimate counseling. Seeking help can be constructive. But to smear my partner haphazardly is a miserable practice.

When the Bible speaks of the woman of noble character, it says, "Her husband has full confidence in her" (Proverbs 31:11). He doesn't have to worry about what she is saying or doing. The Bible also tells us: "A gossip betrays a confidence, but a trustworthy man keeps a secret" (Proverbs 11:13).

Flexercise

1. Do you feel safe at home? Why?
2. When you have a new idea, is your partner more likely to encourage you or discourage you?
3. How free do you feel to be yourself?
4. How successful have you been at putting your relationship above your own interests?
5. How concerned are you that your husband or wife might have an affair? Explain.
6. On a scale of 1 to 10, how relaxed are you with your spouse? How might this be improved?

Compromise is not a dirty word.   **12**

Marriage Is a Swap Meet

*M*arshall and Jennie are two of my favorite people. They have developed a neat marriage relationship which they continually work at. In the process, this mid-western couple has created a unique way to negotiate.

When they go out on a date, they frequently use a point system to plan their evening. If they talk about going to a movie, each partner indicates how much he wants to see that film. The points have to total 100 or else they look for something else to do. If Marshall says his interest is seventy but Jennie's interest is only ten, they don't go. Sometimes it's sixty-forty and the light is green. Should Jenny hit ninety and Marshall register a mere ten, they take in the event because it means so much to one of them that the other partner wants to make it happen.

Often they use the same method to select a restaurant. Do they feel like Mexican or Chinese? The tally might be thirty-thirty on Mexican that evening, so they head for the Chopstick Palace.

Many loving couples have discovered schemes which allow give and take to operate with a minimum of arguments. Creative negotiations provide a maximum of marriage satisfaction.

Pat and I have seen some dates turn into disasters because we couldn't agree on where to go. We have left the house to go out and eat, driven around for forty-five minutes and retreated home frustrated, angry and miserable.

The conversation would begin innocently enough. "You pick the restaurant. I'll take you anywhere you want to go." To which she would reply, "Oh, you know I like to eat anywhere."

You would think that little exchange would be the beginning of a beautiful evening. But more often it was the start of a cold silent standoff. No one was willing to say, "Let's eat at Benny's."

Necessity forced us to form a system. Often one of us will say, "I'd be happy with fish or Italian. You choose which one." This allows the first person to venture some preference without feeling too pushy. The second person then knows whichever he chooses, the selection will be close to what his partner had in mind.

Decisions become safe which greatly increases the possibility of a happy evening together. And it certainly beats having both of us go into the dumper for the evening.

Swap Meets Are Fair

One reason couples have so much trouble accepting negotiating games like these is because many think it is a sign of defeat. We imagined that marriage would be mostly doves cooing, and we would just naturally meet each other's needs. Put that concept into the trash masher. Marriage is not a morning glory. The petals do not automatically open every day in beautiful symmetry.

Some of the key words to a wholesome marriage are:

negotiating	exchange
bargaining	swapping
trading	give and take
deals	entice
compromise	concession
reciprocal	barter

Too often Christians come from a background where compromise was a dirty word. We believed you did things because they were "right" or because you were "told to." If all of life could be handled that way, then "deals" wouldn't be necessary. But in the intimate world of marriage, smart couples either learn the word *concession* or they usually learn the word *misery*.

Every summer Rich took his wife, Nicole, to Washington state where her mother lived. Rich hated every minute of it. The trip meant one solid week of sitting in an overheated, over-doilied living room visiting with Mother.

Rich frequently made suggestions on how he might better enjoy this annual foray to the coast. Why didn't they take an afternoon and go fishing? How about a ride down to see the Mariners play ball? A one-day trip to the mountains sounded appealing.

Nicole said no to all of this. "After all," she protested, "Mother would never understand. She would think you don't like her."

They stayed at home, looked at photo albums and went to bed at nine o'clock. Rich and Nicole did that for ten years until Rich made the announcement: "I'm not going to visit your mother anymore. You fly out, spend the week discussing her violets and then catch the plane home."

And Rich never went again—until the funeral.

That happens all over the country and it's entirely unnecessary. Nicole didn't know how to bargain. All she could see was her goal. If she had made a few deals with Rich, they could have spent many summers paddling around the Puget Sound *and* seeing Mother.

> **When we ask our spouse to do something that we know he doesn't choose to do, we are obligated to bait the hook—if at all possible.**

Sometimes we can't lighten the load. We may have to ask him to go along, grin and bear it. That can be part of the marriage experience. But whenever possible we need to supply gobs of added incentives.

We Make Deals With Friends

Sooner or later the question comes up, "Why do we treat our friends better than we treat our spouses?" Finally I figured out the answer. It's because we have to.

If we dealt with our friends the way many of us deal with our mates, we wouldn't have any friends. No kidding.

When I go to a ball game with a friend, I am anxious that we work out the accommodations amicably. I want him to think well of me and I want him to go again. I tend to be generous, thoughtful, considerate.

I say such civilized things as:

"Do you mind if we leave early?"

"I'd be happy to drive."

"Let me put that stuff in the trunk for you."

"Want me to get you a hot dog?"

If I said half of those things to my wife, she might think I was speaking a foreign language.

Why do we treat our friends better than our mates? Because we don't want to risk losing our friends.

We learn to be adept negotiators outside the home. *Enticement, concession, barter* are all fair words in business, companionship and even sports. But in marriage we become hard-nosed and inflexible.

The Boom-Boom Communicator vs. the Pump-Primer

You meet them every day. They are the people who believe that if they want something badly, they need to express themselves in loud, stern (even mean) terms. They say clever things like:

"I'm going to the ball game and I don't care who likes it."

"Mark Friday night off the calendar; my soap is on."

"We're taking the family to Florida for Christmas; better tell them."

They are masters at closing a conversation down. Void of any negotiating skills, they lead with their chins and dare anyone to argue about it. They are the "Boom-Boom Communicators."

There is another group which feels just as strongly but their philosophy is quite different. They think that if you want something, you had better marshal your best negotiating skills. They set about devising ways to prime the pump.

Both approaches may get their way. But the come-down-hard tactic leaves bodies strewn all over the street. The prime-the-pump method pulls everyone up on the bandwagon.

The Boom-Boom communicator comes in the room and announces crisply, "I'm not going." This dares anyone to fight him. The Pump-Primer says, "This trip presents a problem to me." They have invited a discussion.

Boom-Boomers doubt their ability to negotiate. Pump-Primers believe they can find a way for everyone to get along. Pump-Primers appear to have happier marriages.

Male and Female Traders

At the risk of becoming stereotypical, let's consider if men and women use different bargaining chips. The answer is that they seem to on many but not all occasions.

If we drew bargain chips, they probably would look like this:

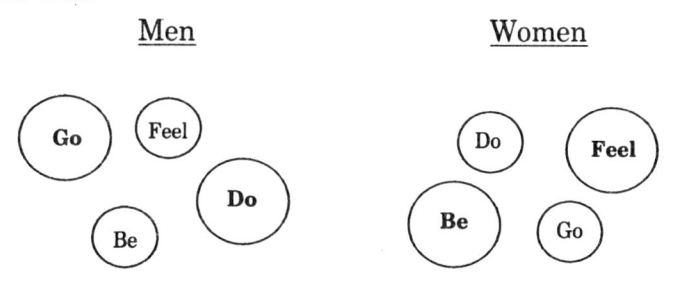

<u>Men</u>　　　　　　　　　　<u>Women</u>

(Go) (Feel)　　　　　　　(Do) (Feel)
  (Do)
(Be)　　　　　　　　　　(Be) (Go)

I say this hesitantly because it could lead to a great deal of misunderstanding. But this does appear to be the case. If you want to bargain with men they *tend* to want "Go" and "Do" chips more often than they want "Feel" and "Be" chips. Women *tend* to want the opposite.

A successful bargain with a man is likely to sound like: "Why don't we spend Friday evening at home giving back rubs, and Saturday night I'll go to the auto races with you?"

Men are less comfortable with *feeling chips* like the ones below, but they may be blue chips for women.

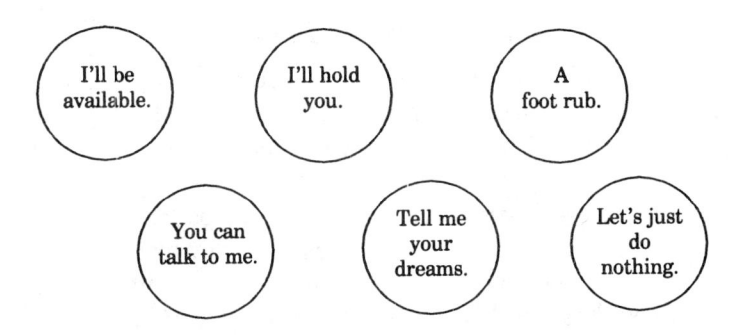

- I'll be available.
- I'll hold you.
- A foot rub.
- You can talk to me.
- Tell me your dreams.
- Let's just do nothing.

Everyone must study and know his spouse. Which chips usually work best for him? On a given day the chips may be entirely different. A sensitive marriage partner stays alert and makes the appropriate moves.

Threats Make Terrible Bargaining Chips

Too many of us are familiar with the bargaining process as a negative approach. We have said such poetic phrases as:

"If you don't go with me, you can fix your own supper."

"If I can't go fishing, you can paint your own porch."

Those are bargaining chips, but they are threatening. Some of us, unfortunately, do not believe in positive chips but are in love with negative ones.

We often think a person should do what is "right" in our eyes and if they don't, that person should receive pain.

Some chips should be negative. Not all motivation can be positive. A good negative chip might be: "If you insist on going to Vancouver for our vacation, that will financially eliminate our skiing trip later"; or "If you keep overloading the washing machine and it breaks down, we won't be able to buy another one." With a spouse, though, positive chips will go much further than any destructive threat.

Positive chips are a new experiment for many. However, we have to take a risk and use them if we want a healthy relationship.

Bargains Are Not Bribes

Bribes and deals are closely related but they are not the same. Some partners will reject the idea of bargains because they are suspicious that the process is evil. Not to worry.

If the company you work for gives you a paycheck, they are not offering a bribe. The check is a reward and an incentive. You earned the money and they want you to return on Monday and do some more of what you have been doing.

A bribe is underhanded and sinister. Bargaining chips are motivational tools designed to promote good behavior and keep it coming. The old theory that people should behave well without compensation or recognition is idealistic and risky.

It's hard to go wrong if we keep the goodies coming.

Paul's Plea for Exchange

Sometimes the apostle Paul was one tight-jawed leader in no uncertain terms. But, he also recognized the importance of making trades. The believers in Corinth often frustrated him because of the lousy behavior and lack of respect for this outstanding Christian.

Can you believe that this clear-thinking, steel-trap mind makes a plea to the Corinthians that they swap affection for each other? Read carefully what he tells them:

> We have spoken freely to you, Corinthians, and opened wide our hearts to you. We are not withholding our affection from you, but you are withholding yours from us. As a fair exchange—I speak as to my children—open wide your hearts also (2 Corinthians 6:11-13).

That old softy. He asks them to swap affection on the basis that he gave it first. Paul knew how to offer up bargaining chips.

I don't know for sure whether Paul was married or not but he had the makings of a great husband. He might have said, "Honey, don't forget, I take out the trash, wash out the gourds and trim the wicks. If that should make you feel like rubbing my back, who am I to stop you?"

Flexercise

1. Do you have a system which allows you to compromise over a date or a trip? How do you do it?

2. Do you treat friends better than your spouse? How? Why?

3. Are you a Boom-Boom communicator or a Pump-Primer? How might you improve?

4. What bargaining chips do you enjoy? What bargaining chips does your spouse enjoy?

Almost every argument falls into one of three categories.

13

What Do We Argue About?

*I*f you never argue, you should get the "Happy Couple Award." I find it hard to believe that there are marriage partners who don't argue, but every now and again I meet someone who insists it's true. If they say they don't, who am I to say they do?

But inside, quietly, I am suspicious that something is happening which they may not recognize.

Possibly they are *arguing and calling it something else*. They may disagree, debate, express their opinions, challenge each other or play some other game of semantics.

Many couples *argue silently through indirect messages*. Bob and Leona never raise their voices. They send each other ugly stares, give cold shoulders and share an icy bed, but they never do get around to a verbal argument.

Often *one partner is too empty to argue*. We see couples where one partner has no genius to offer. Either he feels he has nothing worth saying or he has given up trying. After having his views pulverized for years, this person sees no point in venturing his opinion.

Some may be confused about arguing, but the rest of us argue and we know it. It's crystal clear. Some of us have windburns on our foreheads from the times our partner has expressed his or her sentiments.

Arguing Can Be Healthy

Arguing is the normal route of most marriage partners. Couples who have found constructive ways to disagree tend to have a richer, more satisfying union. But arguments that rev up and become mere screaming bouts, create perilous situations. Should the couple withdraw and refuse to express their differences, they squirrel away their feelings and risk emotional injury.

But a solid, constructive, sane argument is hard to beat for marriage enrichment.

The reason we have to say this is because so many of us have unrealistic expectations. If we watch television or movies we gather the impression that couples argue all the time. That atmosphere is created because most stories center around conflict. By watching so many stories we might get the idea that marriage is continuous turmoil. That is extreme and untrue.

On the other hand, we may have been taught that all our conflicts are resolvable and, consequently, Christian marriage could live above serious disagreement. That is generally a fairy tale.

Conflict is normal.
Conflict is healthy.
Conflict is creative.
Conflict is inevitable.
Conflict is expanding.

> It is possible for marriage partners to say, "We don't agree. Good! Let's see how we are going to work this out."

What Do We Argue About?

We have asked hundreds of married people: "If you and your partner were going to have an argument, what are the three things you are most likely to argue over?"

We also asked single adults and children: "What do you think married couples argue about the most?"

Their responses were almost unanimous. Most of us argue over the same things and practically everyone outside of our marriage knows exactly what we are tussling over. We grew up in homes where our parents struggled over these same problems. And now those traits trickled down and are part of our relationships.

The three things we argue over the most are:

- Money
- Children
- Sex/Time

Occasionally, the couples we asked differed from this trio, but not often. Someone would put down "politics" or "baking pies," but rarely.

Why Do We Argue Over These Issues?

If a subject is static and impersonal, we probably don't argue about it much. When was the last time you and your spouse slept in separate rooms because you couldn't agree on whether we should have entered the First World War? Who of us has sulked the evening away over the selection of the state bird?

The big three are highly personal and they reflect the value system we brought into the relationship. They are sensitive issues and are close to the core of who we are.

These three are also volatile. They are not static and it is their very movement which makes them explosive. Only fools handle explosives roughly without respect for their destructive properties.

Number One Is Money

Almost everyone argues over money. In most cases the arguing has nothing to do with the amount of money we have or don't have. If we doubled our income next year, we would still argue over the little paper menace. A famous entertainment family said they fight over money all the time; the only difference is that in their home you merely add a couple of zeroes after each figure.

There is plenty of reason to believe that the present generation argues over money more than their grandparents. In his book about finding meaning in life, Dr. Paul Welter notes a definite shift. Twenty years ago over 80 percent of college students interviewed identified their goal in life as "developing a meaningful life." In recent years most students saw their goal in life as "being very well-off financially."[1]

This new trend may be significantly responsible for much of the tension we find in present-day marriages. This tension will continue as long as certain attitudes are present.

1. We Believe Possessions Make the Person

If the only way I can feel good abut myself is to own things, then the battle for objects will continue forever. The premise that possessions make the person is false and will never satisfy. The chase for finances will never end since the goal cannot be reached. All of us know this and, then again, almost none of us know this.

We are chasing the carrot which is tied to a string on a pole which is latched on to our backs. The carrot dangles one foot in front of our mouth *and always will*. Unfortunately, we choose to believe that if we run faster we could catch the carrot.

2. We Live on the Financial Edge

When we get a raise, we buy a bigger house. When we get close to paying off the car, we purchase another one. We tie into a philosophy of money which *guarantees that we cannot win*. Since we believe we should create financial tension, we likely will do that throughout our working years.

Call this "wall pushing." We consider it our duty to live just a few dollars beyond our means. If our finances come dangerously close to our goals, we respond by moving our goals farther out of range.

Anyone with this attitude toward money should invest heavily in aspirin companies.

3. We See Money as a Sign of God's Blessing

The "God wants you rich" philosophy remains popular despite the fact that the New Testament teaches just the opposite. As long as we believe that we and God are in cahoots to get us a condominium in Aspen, we will tie our spiritual lives and our prosperity together.

A more biblical approach is to say: (1) God may allow me to purchase a condominium. If He does, I am grateful. (2) If God permits this, He also warns me of the temptations and pitfalls which go with it.

To be honest, the Bible tells us to watch out for material gain:

> But godliness with contentment is great gain. For we brought nothing into the world, and we can take nothing out of it. But if we have food and clothing, we will be content with that. People who want to get rich fall into temptation and a trap and into many foolish and harmful desires that plunge men into ruin and destruction. For the love of money is a root of all kinds of evil. Some people, eager for money, have wandered from the faith and pierced themselves with many griefs (1 Timothy 6:6-10).

4. We Define Each Other as Spenders and Savers

Few couples agree on the rate at which they spend money. It almost can't be done. The couples I have talked to about this have explained the built-in problem.

When he sees her spending money, the natural reaction is for him to become frightened and start to save money. If he spends big bucks on cars and toys, she is likely to react by saying, "We're going to go broke." She then turns frugal and begins tucking some cash into cracks around the house or at her bank.

Rarely do you see a couple both spending at an equal breakneck speed. Since they spend at different rates, friction is practically a given.

All of us need to know that it is normal for us to argue over money. If we develop a budget and discuss our individual attitudes toward spending, saving, giving and earning, we are more likely to reach a peaceful method of handling finances.

Number Two Is Children

Even grandparents put this down as a major topic for argument. They bicker over whether their forty-year-old married son should quit his job and go to work for a fast food company. When your children are pre-schoolers, it's hard to imagine that thirty-five years later you and your spouse would raise your voices over them. But parents do.

How often have you heard a couple say, "We never have disagreed over the children"? Not a likely picture.

There are several primary reasons we argue over the children. Remember, these causes are *normal* to most of us.

1. We Come From Different Backgrounds

No matter if we come from similar backgrounds, we still come from different backgrounds. Even if we attended the same church, school, neighborhood and took aerobic swimming together, we still experienced separate family values.

Should children

talk at the table?	watch detective shows?
chew gum?	have daily devotions?
go to bed early?	take piano lessons?
listen to loud music?	say the word "crud"?
climb trees?	wear make up?

Each parent has carved out a sense of values in relation to his own children. The other parent, understandably, has chiseled out his also. Neither person is likely to surrender his most prized beliefs easily.

The majority of our specific values are unknown to us until we actually have children. We don't really know how we feel about Johnny climbing trees until we see our seven-year-old inching his way out onto a shaky branch. We aren't sure how we feel about Suzie driving the car to the next town fifty miles away until she asks us if she can go.

The task of cultivating children calls for compromise and some of us will not know how intransigent we are until the time arrives to make decisions. Humility, patience and teamwork become vital for a couple who dream of getting along.

2. We Place Our Personal Worth in Our Children

Parents who expect their children to serve as trophies are in for a large amount of tension. In order for us to "shine" through our children, we usually have to smudge over whatever goals our children wish to develop.

"You must be terribly proud that your daughter is going to be a dentist," a lady told Arlene.

"Yes, I am," Arlene replied, "but I would have been just as proud of her if she had become a secretary."

Arlene refused to confuse her daughter's job with the daughter herself. Neither did she demand her daughter to find a career which would put an imaginary feather in her mother's imaginary cap.

Parents are more likely to relax and allow their children to make decisions if the parents are not chained to their children's behavior. Acceptance is far more likely to take place when parent and child are counted as individuals.

How many boys are hounded into sports?
How many girls are pushed into dating?
How many children are guided into the business?
How many young people are expected to go to college?
How many children are forced into trumpet lessons?

Too many.

3. Children Are Dynamic

If children were china cabinets, they would be easy to agree on. China cabinets neither grow nor move. We can take our time discussing what goes in them. After a year of checking out paints and stains we might decide to remove the old finish and slap on a new one over the exposed wood.

With children we do not have the luxury we have with inanimate objects. Children keep wiggling, moving, sliding, learning, running, bouncing, asking, leaping, pestering, smiling, jiggling, calling, begging, pushing, pulling and throwing up.

China cabinets don't do that.

Animate objects, like children, have a mind of their own and do not control so easily. As they grow older, they become even less easily controlled.

Because children are alive, their parents can *expect* to argue about them. That's normal.

Why Do We Have Children Anyway?

Don't ask yourself why did you have children in the first place. If there was ever a perfect example of a moot question, that has to be it. You have the children. What do you want to see happen to them now?

Take a piece of paper and a pencil (both are great for getting organized). Sit down with your spouse and make a list of what you want to see happen in the lives of your children. Reach as much agreement as possible and try to respect your differences.

Make the goals general such as:

be an independent thinker
know about Jesus Christ
be responsible
be considerate
think positively
respect authority

Many parents have little idea of what would go on their list. Once you reach general agreement on the goals, *begin to plot together* on how you are most likely to reach these targets.

Without any concept of what the targets are, parents shoot in all directions and occasionally hit each other.

Number Three Is Sex and Time

The fact that sex and time tied for third place is no accident. At first I was mystified, but the couples I talked to explained how they are related.

Women tend to see time as sex. If her husband sits on the couch with his leg next to hers, that is a sexual experience. It is not a substitute for sex, but touching is part of the total picture.

If the husband is seldom around, the couple most likely will have sex in short, frantic shots. Those "quickies" usually satisfy the male more than the female. She believes in foreplay and that buildup takes time. He thinks foreplay is the sound of a zipper.

Of course, this is not always true. Sometimes she is drooling right after supper and sometimes he needs the big buildup. But the pattern more often requires time for her and a wink for him.

I refused to believe this for years, but I surrender. Women are more likely to see sex as an experience. Men tend to see sex as an event. He wants to have sex at halftime and then get up to watch the rest of the 49ers game. She likes to have sex and then lie in bed and be held. He doesn't understand what all of the "holding" is about. He figures they already "did it."

Women do like a buildup, and a buildup takes time. Men who bowl three nights a week don't have a chance.

The remedy again lies in communication. Two marriage partners can sit down and each say, "Honey, what can I do to make your sex life satisfying?" And when your partner answers, do it.

As long as our sex temperament is different—however it is different—we have the potential for friction. Communication will reduce that disagreement.

We have no reason to fear a civil argument. It is no sin to disagree. Arguing helps clear the air and moves us forward to an understnading and a solution. Healthy is the couple who have learned to talk out their frustrations.

Flexercise

1. If you added a fourth thing to your list of arguments, what would it be?

2. What one change would reduce your arguments over money?

3. What one change would reduce your arguments over children?

4. What one change would reduce your arguments over sex and time?

---

1. Paul Welter, *Counseling and the Search for Meaning* (Waco, TX: Word Publishing, 1987), p. 29.

If you think marriage is rough,
wait until you try divorce.

14

The Six Myths of Divorce

*D*ivorce appears to be getting a great deal of good press lately. Everybody seems to be doing it. We don't want to say much against it because the person sitting next to us has probably been divorced – at least once.

A major emphasis has been placed on how to heal people after the divorce. No one wants to judge, condemn or cast any aspersions on the divorce procedure.

That makes some sense. After all, divorced people are hurting enough as it is. However, we do need to raise our hand and make one suggestion. Everyone should know that divorce isn't exactly a day at the beach.

> **A divorced man with children said, "Divorce is the funeral that never ends."**

As married couples are waking up to that reality, some are calling out for the church to do something about it. They are insisting on more sermons, more classes, more premarital counseling. They see a disease sweeping across marriage and leaving couples like corpses rotting on the ground.

Among those who are calling the loudest for action are the child-victims of divorce. They are *afraid* that their marriages will suffer the same fate as their parents. And they don't want anyone to go through the pain they have experienced.

Couples with lasting marriages have drawn a line. It is a negative line to be sure but it says, "Divorce is no option." They are ready to try anything else—even if it is miserable—but the thought of divorce is too terrible to consider.

Linda was the kind of girl everyone liked. But since the divorce she had lost some of her sparkle. Her smile looked forced and her eyes were tired.

"If I had only known what divorce is like," she said candidly, "I would have worked a lot harder on the marriage."

That chorus is being sung by thousands who thought they would find happiness through divorce. Those with children are especially discovering that divorce can bring tremendous, lasting pain. Too late they learn the adage: If you think marriage is tough, wait until you try divorce.

No one should tell us how to run our lives, but a few facts might prove helpful. All of us should consider what's on the other side of marriage.

Consider six of the most prevalent myths about divorce.

Myth #1: Immediate Release

The person getting a divorce can't own enough handkerchiefs. No matter what caused the split, heartache is a certain fact. Nights, days, months, possibly years of strain are ahead.

When a person isn't crying, he's usually shaken with guilt. What did he do wrong? Could they have worked it out? Why did they marry in the first place? What have they done to the children?

Even under circumstances that seem black and white, the demon guilt will haunt you. Many brave souls brace themselves to resist it, but hardly anyone escapes.

Most couples are under financial pressure and have convinced themselves that divorce will open new resources.

The opposite is almost always true. Two households will have to be maintained. Many families have to move to lesser neighborhoods and smaller homes. The fantasy of greater prosperity quickly crumbles.

Myth #2: Growing Happiness

While it's true that some experience increased happiness, the majority find greater difficulties as time goes by.

First, they have to pay lawyers, which can cost into the thousands if the separating couple has trouble agreeing. Some settlements are amiable but few are genuinely satisfying.

Second, the court will try to work out a compromise concerning the children, but no plan is ideal. If one person gets custody, the other frequently feels inferior or inadequate. Mothers without custody often feel they cannot fulfill a role they want. Husbands grind at not having control.

Third, financial arrangements might look good at first, but they are seldom adequate. In many cases, the father fails to send child support on time, if at all, and further haggling results. Sometimes the tension never goes away.

"I hate writing that check every month," Chuck said. "The divorce was her idea. Let her support the kid."

Frustrated, the mother asks the law to help her collect the support. She soon finds the authorities ill-equipped to carry it out.

Consider an average mother with two children, divorced after three to five years of marriage. She has a low-income job and often receives the child support check late if at all. Trapped, she faces a terribly hard future.

Myth #3: The Children Are Better Off

This is definitely true in some cases, but most of the time divorce takes its toll on our youth. Except where children are being abused, many would have been better off in their original family unit.

A number of experts believe divided families to be a major cause for the increased number of suicides among college students. These students suffer from the lack of unity and security. Often they distrust relationships and have little faith in their ability to hold a marriage together for themselves. The American bliss of marriage looks like a nightmare to many.

"I don't think I want to get married," a college student recently told me. "Not many hold together and I don't need all that agony."

High school youth fare no better when their parents divorce. They have entered an often turbulent stage of their development. Under the best of conditions they struggle for identity and could use helpful guidance. Instead they watch a major part of their world fall apart.

A high percentage of teenagers express hostility when their parents get divorced. They wonder why anyone would want to bring extra pain into their unstable lives.

For most teens, divorce means less money, less car use, a possible move and turmoil. For some, their college plans must be altered or dropped for the time being, possibly forever. They needed a rock to stand on and it turned to sand. And they're mad about it.

Frequently teenagers see divorce as the ultimate selfish act. They believe their parents owed it to them to keep their act together. Don't be surprised if they hold a grudge at one or both parents possibly for years.

With younger children the problems can be even more serious. Many are likely to blame themselves for the divorce. As Robin said, "I have wondered for twenty-six years how I caused my parents' divorce."

In many cases no one discusses the divorce with the child. They are left to imagine what caused it. Since most of their world revolves around themselves, they often assume they made it happen. If no one fills in the blanks, they will try to supply their own logic to the situation.

One of the child's greatest fears is abandonment. To have one parent abandon him or her opens a floodgate of possibilities which frighten him.

It's true that some children are better off because of a divorce. However, many others are hurt deeply and remain bruised for many years.

Myth #4: It's No One Else's Business

All of us like to feel independent, but that's seldom the case. We each touch other lives as they touch us. It's the natural result of those who dare to love.

Divorce usually causes a circle of pain. Parents are affected by the agony they see when their grown child divorces. Frequently they cry together. A large number of parents contribute financially. Some open their homes and let their children move in, possibly with one or two grandchildren. Uncles, aunts, grandparents, brothers and sisters can be hurt in ways that we might not have imagined.

Friends are also caught in the wave. As Ron explained it, "I never dreamed how much it hurt to watch someone close to you go through a divorce." Pressed in the middle, friends are torn between the two sides, struggling to keep their balance without hurting anyone.

Myth #5: Things Will Calm Down

Fortunately there is some truth to this hope, but for some the pain remains throughout life. "Every time we trade the kids back and forth, we yell at each other over nothing," was Judy's experience. "We can't seem to talk about anything without getting angry."

How many weddings have you attended where the divorced parents of the bride or groom barely tolerated each other? Their wounds did not heal.

Many people remarry into step-parenting situations which are extremely uncomfortable. Step-parenting can be a miserable readjustment.

Because some divorces are not handled well, we see children who resent one parent. Forced to choose sides they remain bitter for years, even decades.

Myth #6: At Least I Am Rid of Him/Her

If a couple has children, a person will probably never be fully rid of his former spouse. The desire to make a clean sweep and get him or her behind them is usually a fantasy.

Naturally there will be the normal contact over child support and children's visitation rights. Special occasions can be far worse. This is where I see divorcees. They sit in different parts of the auditorium at their child's band recital. They stand at the far corners of the parking lot after graduation. When the child is sick, they pass uncomfortably in the hospital corridors not knowing what to say to each other. At the child's wedding, the divorced parents jockey for positions over who sits where and who enters the church first. Funerals for grandparents or other relatives become tension-packed and often guilt-ridden.

There is no magic wand which makes a person disappear simply because you divorced him or her.

There are people who have risen to new happiness because of their divorces. That is an inescapable fact. However, the benefits of divorce are often exaggerated. Before a person asks the courts to end a marriage, he should weigh the consequences. Thousands of couples wish they had gone back and made the ship sail instead of gutting it.

If you think your marriage is hard, wait until you try divorce.

Hopefully couples will do more than simply declare their opposition to divorce. More constructively, they will take positive steps to build up their marriage strengths. Many began by throwing divorce out as an option.

And Yet Another Myth

As optimists, we like to think we are the exceptions to all the gory scenarios we have just mentioned. Civilized,

Christian couples such as ourselves should be able to work out a "friendly" divorce. None of us wants to hurt each other.

Maybe your husband has said that if you two should ever split he would want you to have the house, the car, the cat, the c.d.'s, alimony, child support, cost of living increases and he will clean your gutters three times every fall.

What could sound more amicable than that? Isn't this the day of joint petitions, no-fault divorces, special mediators and mature separations? Does one church have a divorce service where the couple declares their independence in front of the entire congregation?

Come back to reality. Despite the apparent ease with which we can be divorced, only six percent of divorces are filed jointly. The rest engage in some form of fighting it out. Women usually file for the divorce (twice as often as men). Often the generous spouse who offered you the farm has now seen his or her lawyer and has opted for tough negotiations.

Friendly divorces may sound good. So do ice cream mountains, orange drink fountains and money trees.

Flexercise

1. Why don't you divorce your spouse?

2. How are your divorced friends with children doing?

3. What measures are you taking to make divorce less likely?

If we allow them, children can make wonderful contributions to our marital happiness.

15

Because of the Children

*T*here is no single reason why marriages last. Like a good rope, a relationship needs many strands to make it strong.

The people we asked about marriage had a firm conviction that children contributed to their marriage longevity. Often they expressed this in the healthiest of terms:

"We cared enough about each other, our children and our grandchildren to always work things out. Though we came from dysfunctional families, we believe it is God's plan for our lives to try to help our family be whole and healthy."

"We have concern for children."

"Our children like it this way."

"Love — love of God, love of husband, love of family."

"I have two sons who I'd never want to hurt."

"We have good children."

"My wife's and daughters' happiness is before mine."

"We believe in commitment for our children's and grandchildren's sake in the future."

If children are the only reason a couple "hangs" in there, the marriage is sitting on a shaky foundation. But no one needs to apologize for feelings of love, loyalty and concern for their children. There is much to be said for providing a good example, a safe harbor, secure experiences, stability and basic happiness. Children need to see love up close—the love their parents have for each other and the love they have for their children. Children in Christian homes deserve a firsthand view of spiritual reality and Christian values at work.

Since we brought children into this world, we have a responsibility to them. *Responsibility* is a valid and noble word. No one need feel embarrassed to say he takes his responsibilities seriously. None of us should be ashamed to admit we made reasonable sacrifices for the sake of our children. All of us can feel good that there are parents who still think this way.

Neglect is an empty and ugly word. Neglect suggests such putrid concepts as spoiled, wasted and abandoned. If you know someone who was brought up in a family where the feelings were extremely ambivalent, you probably understand the severity of the problem. Not knowing whether your parents love you will bruise your very soul. To have been abused physically or emotionally creates an empty, hollow feeling which can remain for a lifetime.

Couples who believe their children are a contributing factor to their marriage should be praised and not pitied. If, however, children are the *only* reason they stay married, the couple is missing the great satisfaction which a good relationship could provide. They still have time to pump new life into their love for each other.

Compassion for Our Children

Caring about our children is a normal response. Parents are supposed to have that attitude.

"As a father has compassion on his children, so the Lord has compassion on those who fear him" (Psalm 103:13).

The parent who goes for marriage counseling because he or she doesn't want to hurt his children should be given airline discounts and a free pool pass. Instead, they are frequently ridiculed for not putting their own interests first.

Employees who refuse to move in order to keep their children's roots strong might be dismissed from the company. What they should receive is a raise for being an outstanding human being.

Many adults who were the victims of their parents' divorce are saying, "I will not put my children through the pain I went through," and they are caring for their own marriages. That attitude doesn't always work, but it is an added incentive for millions to make the most of their marriages.

Recently, it has become popular to say that couples *should* divorce "for the sake of the children." Divorce can help some children—but rarely.

Studies indicate that *most* children have trouble coping with the divorce of their parents. And for many, that pain only increases with time. Ten years after the divorce a large number of children have *more* difficulty coping rather than less. Time is not the great healer that many of us hoped it would be.

Children frequently feel abandoned by at least one parent in a divorce. They distrust relationships. If the father is perceived to be the one who caused the divorce, often daughters are reluctant to trust men when they attempt to establish marriages for themselves.

Under these circumstances it is understandable that often child-victims of divorce have trouble stabilizing their own marriages.

It is hard to fault parents who work doubly hard to revitalize their marriage "for the sake of the children."

Children Bring Something to the Marriage

Children should not be just one of those dreary reasons couples "stick it out." If we allow them, children can add a tremendous amount of love, joy and pleasure to a marriage relationship.

For too long we have thought of children as blank pages. We think of them as helpless, empty beings waiting for us to write our marks on their characters. But have we stopped to consider how the child contributes to our marriage? A child is able to add to our relationship by:

1. Exchanging Love

Children need what we have to offer. If we permit ourselves, we can overflow with love to our child who is a ready and willing receptacle. In turn, the child supplies love which allows us to keep our larder full. The best way to keep love is to give it away.

2. Add Meaning

Our children keep us from becoming too selfish. The message on their faces says, "Sports cars are not the most important part of life." "Freedom is not the goal of our existence."

3. Illustrate Faith

Trust, belief and hope are etched early in the lives of children and shine as an example when our faith falters. As parents, we understand more completely what it meant for God to sacrifice a child for us. We have greater appreciation for a heavenly Father's love because we have experience with earthly fathers.

4. Understanding of Loyalty

Responsibility is an intra-family exercise. We can learn loyalty to the people we love because we see the need in our children. We are also likely to see their loyalty to us. Interdependence keeps us close to the people who should count the most.

Children help marriages on two levels. First, the love of and love for children give a couple mortar. It helps hold the bricks in place. Second, a couple realizes that they "owe" their children something. (And *owe* is a word which mature adults can handle.) They are obligated to provide a decent environment, emotional stability and a fair shot at life. Couples maintain a sense of accomplishment and purpose when they earnestly attempt to supply these qualities.

"Ten years ago I would have left if it hadn't been for the kids," Jim declared. "But now we are as happy as chipmunks together."

How often have we heard that? Jim should give each of his children a wall plaque of appreciation. They played a substantial role in giving Jim and his wife, Toni, an extra decade of marriage, companionship and satisfaction.

On the other hand, how many couples have started cutting ties with their children as a prelude to leaving their partners?

"Jerry suddenly stopped playing with Andy," Colleen remembered. "He even stopped calling him by his name. Jerry called him 'the kid.' That's how I knew he was getting serious about leaving. It was almost as if he had to disown his boy so he could disown me."

Another woman said, "Charlie would start saying these stupid things like, 'A lot of children are better off without their father. I know people whose parents divorced and they are lots tougher for it.' So I'd say, 'Charlie, what are you trying to say? Do you think your girls would honestly be better off without you?' "

At some point many of us asked this pivotal question: "Am I going to improve my marriage because of the children or am I going to use them to help us separate?"

It is not enough to say, "We despise each other but we stick it out for the kids." That statement is inviting terrible pain for everyone involved. A better approach is, "Since our miserable relationship could have a gruesome impact on our children, *we have all the more reason* to turn our marriage into a loving partnership."

Vital Connection

None of can afford to be disconnected. Each of us needs an official or unofficial support system. For most couples, children play a significant role in stabilizing even the most disheveled of us. If you doubt that, talk to middle-aged couples who not only have empty nests but also have watched their children move far away. They must find more friends or they risk coming apart.

Whenever possible, parent and child need to maintain their connection. Both the child and the parent are more likely to keep their balance if their extended family cares what happens to them.

The biblical principle is clear. Parents need to work at the love they have for their children. Even when it doesn't come easily.

"They can train the younger women to love their husbands and children" (Titus 2:4).

It is important to everyone in the family that we maintain a love for each other. In the long run, individual family members supply a portion of the mortar which holds us together.

Children as Resources

One of our grown children recently looked me in the eye over coffee and said, "Dad, how is your love life?" I shrugged it off as a feeble attempt at humor only to have her repeat it. "No, Dad, I really mean it. How is your love life?"

> **Children are more interested in what is going on in their parents' lives, more aware of what is happening and often more able to help than we may appreciate.**

What would happen if a mother said to her five-year-old, "Your dad and I haven't been talking much lately"? Would you be surprised to hear the youngster say, "Why don't you bake him a pie?" Would you hate to admit that the child was right?

What if you said to your ten-year-old daughter, "Boy, has your mom been grouchy lately"? Would you hear something like, "Everybody gets grumpy sometimes. Let's do the dishes for her tonight."

The answers were correct and even obvious, but we needed to hear someone else say them to motivate us to action. That help often comes from the child we wanted to keep out of the problem.

If children are accepted as human beings, they know a great deal about what it takes to get along with people.

Flexercise

1. What do your children add to your marriage?

2. What do we "owe" our children?

3. Have you ever shared a marital problem with a child? How did he react?

16 Have your expectations about marriage been met?

The Calculated Marriage

This is the day of the calculated marriage. Young couples are less likely to become love struck, throw all caution to the wind and run helter-skelter into a permanent relationship. While love is still strong, it may not be as blind as it used to be.

Everyone who gets married has expectations. And we hope to see our dreams come true. The more dreams that become reality, the more satisfied each spouse will feel. If marriage is nothing like you expected, the experience is usually a bummer.

The calculated marriage has some great strengths. Each partner can fully express his goals and aspirations such as:

Where do we want to live?
How can *her* career goals be met?
How many children are manageable?
Why will we have children?
Will we have children?
How will we worship and serve?
How will our finances be handled?
How will we share responsibility?

Marriages in the past were more likely to have well-defined roles. After the wedding service, each mate seemed to slide into his long-accepted concept of marriage. Today

The Calculated Marriage

men and women have become aware that each partner is a person. Personhood demands that we discuss and work out our expectations.

> **Relationships that are all heart have their problems.**

Couples led only by their hearts tend to make silly decisions and try to rearrange the pieces later. Relationships that are all head need their share of antacids, too. When everything is mathematical, computerized and data-banked, you half expect to get a proposal over your fax machine and leave your reply with an answering service.

Fortunately, there is a happy middle. Smart couples are giving their hearts away and bringing their brains with them.

"What am I supposed to do?" Crystal wondered aloud. "I have my degree and a good job. Am I supposed to pull up stakes, go wherever he wants and take any job I can get?"

Whether they are engaged or have been married for ten years, couples that last discuss their expectations. They try to agree as much as possible and each person works to make dreams come true.

Kay and Bill Orr have been fun to watch. Bill worked hard to help Kay run for and become governor of Nebraska. He had a successful career with an insurance company and seemed tickled to move into the state mansion with his wife.

Soon after being elected, Governor Orr accompanied her husband to an insurance convention where she was just another conventioneer's wife. I can picture her attending a session on how to help your husband in his career. My mind sees her at an evening party wearing a funny hat and listening to old golf jokes.

At least in the newspapers their relationship looks satisfying. Each partner supports the expectations of the other.

Calculated marriages are not just for working couples. Women at home, students and retired folks also benefit from calculated marriages. Everyone has a right and a need to decide what he wants in life and aim for it.

Calculations Change

Calculating our marriages doesn't mean we have to sign a contract which guarantees we will never leave Baltimore, or strike an agreement that promises we try out for the ballet. Times change. People change more. God might open new doors for us. Occasionally we have to sit down and add it all up again.

It's just nice to know both of us will be treated equally in the equation.

Lee Iacocca said when he married the second time he assumed his new bride would move to Detroit. That seemed like a given since he was president of Chrysler. However, the new Mrs. Iacocca just as firmly assumed they would establish their home in New York.

Both seemed so confident in their assumptions that they failed to resolve the matter until after they became married.

Yesterday's assumptions will not work in today's world. We must begin with the premise that life is different today. Then we move to the conclusion that life will continue to change after we get married.

If we have discussed where we want to live, the subject is not final. In a few years a similar discussion will have to be held again and, at a later time, maybe again. We must type the word *change* into our computers and never erase it.

"He told me I could follow my nursing career," Jill was exasperated. "But how can I? Every couple of years we move and I have to start all over again. This isn't what Jeff promised."

But what kind of pressure is Jeff facing? The pressures in his career have left him just as frustrated. He feels there is no alternative but to move around.

The Calculated Marriage

The solution needs to be found in mutual calculation. Things are changing for Jeff and he feels out of control. He believes that if he doesn't move, he will fall apart. At the same time Jill sees herself disintegrating every time they relocate.

Expectations have to be outlined for short periods of time. They then must be renegotiated like contracts.

According to Your Latest Calculations

Since calculated marriages must be refigured periodically, take a few minutes and add yours up. Do not ask what your expectations used to be, rather what are they today.

1. What do you want for your children?
2. What do you want for your marital relationship?
3. What are your financial dreams?
4. What are your spiritual goals?
5. What are your social expectations?
6. Where would you like to vacation?
7. Where would you like to live?
8. Where would you like to work?
9. What interpersonal skill would you like to improve?
10. How would you like to serve others?

As you go through this checklist, try to answer each expectation in one or two sentences. Ask your spouse to join you. What have you learned about the *current you*? What did you learn about your *current spouse*?

Have you and your spouse successfully calculated your marriage? Remember,

1. Calculated marriages are heavy on spelling out expectations.

2. They are willing to renegotiate.

3. They accept change as inevitable.

4. They see a large number of their expectations met.

5. They are willing to sacrifice a reasonable amount of themselves to the relationship.

6. They see each other as equal in the calculation.

No marriage is adequately calculated if only one partner has his expectations met. In a truly fulfilled relationship, each mate possesses a high degree of satisfaction.

Flexercise

1. How have your expectations changed over the years?

2. Do you and your spouse agree on your expectations?

3. Have you learned any secrets on how to negotiate with your partner when it comes to planning goals? What is one?

Happy is the couple who refuses to hold grudges.

17

Let Bygones Be Bygones

"When I told Lennie about the accident, you should have seen the look on his face," Heather said with pleasure. "He walked over, put his arm around me and asked if I was all right. I told him I was, but the grill would never be the same. He just looked at me and said, 'Cars we can fix — you're what really counts.'

"That makes you feel like a million bucks," she continued. "Lennie is always so accepting."

This is the upside of listening to married couples. They have so many healthy, healing and loving stories to tell. Often we major on dramatic, dysfunctional accounts because they make fascinating reading and captivating speaking. But the stories about caring and closeness are the ones we need to connect with. They encourage us in our own pursuit of marital happiness.

Millions of couples are extremely generous with forgiveness. Those are the great love stories. Her husband said something insulting and she decided to throw the remark away, refusing to turn it into hatred. Those are the acts of heroic compassion.

In talking with couples about what makes marriages last, we frequently heard:

"Be willing to forgive and forget."

"Don't let little things build into big things."

"Develop the ability to forgive your spouse even if it's not asked for."

"Have a forgiving attitude toward offenses and get things reconciled quickly."

In many cases, forgiveness did not come quickly or automatically. Frequently, individuals enter marriage with a poor background in forgiving and forgetting. They have seen little modeling in this area. Their parents may have been trained in the skill of grudge holding and guilt manipulation. It's only natural to pick up the practices seen the most.

But this doesn't mean the die is cast forever. In a loving relationship, each of us is capable of learning the craft of releasing our grudges.

Shelly was the kind of wife who kept score. At first she collected offenses and made a mental list of each trespass her husband committed. However, two things happened which allowed Shelly to soften her attitude:

1. She became a Christian and grew to accept the forgiveness of God for her own condition. By experiencing forgiveness in her own life she found it easier to dispense.
2. Shelly saw the sincerity of her husband's forgiveness. At first she did not believe he was really forgiving her. Shelly assumed he was storing her wrongdoings in the back of his mind like she always had.

After several years of marriage and those two special encounters, Shelly found the freedom of forgiveness. There is hope for those who do not have a background in this exercise of grace and mercy.

What about Christians who do not forgive their spouses?

This is a common problem. Forgiveness is not easily dispensed by all Christian partners. One reason may be because this person has not accepted the complete forgiveness of God. If we think God is still angry or disappointed or just a little ticked at us, we have trouble passing on unconditional forgiveness.

When I realize that God has showed His love to me, I will find it easier to be generous with my forgiveness. "Be kind and compassionate to one another, forgiving each other, just as in Christ God forgave you" (Ephesians 4:32).

Some of us have learned to play games with forgiveness. By withholding it we try to make the lack of forgiveness work for us.

We Hold Grudges Like Security Blankets

Have you ever said to yourself, "Sure, I'll forgive her, but not so quickly"? Holding a grudge gives us an emotional high. Our darker side inhales it like drugs.

Sinister feelings are real. People who are uncomfortable with healthy emotions like love and generosity go at a grudge like lizards lick up flies.

We will forgive the person but only after we have enjoyed our perverted form of pleasure.

A mature sense of love will rescue us from delayed forgiveness.

We Preserve a Grudge for Use as Blackmail

If we feel the need to use weapons in our relationship, the refusal to forgive makes up a large part of our arsenal. When we have trouble getting our way through normal channels of persuasion, logic and compromise, we choose to fight dirty. If we seem to be losing the disagreement, we reach back into our emotional bunker and pull out a grudge from the past.

"You never want to do it my way," a blackmail statement might begin. "I gave in to you about the used car and look what happened to that."

She had suggested they buy a Studebaker and he gave in. Soon afterwards the dealership closed down and they had trouble getting parts. Decades later, he still carries that little stink bomb around just in case he needs it.

His blackmail is highly effective because she responds quickly to perceived guilt. The mere mention of Studebaker makes her feel dumb and inadequate. That's why she surrenders and insists that he make the major decisions.

Successful blackmail is dependent on two elements. First, the blackmailer has to be hard-hearted enough to use cruel methods. Second, the blackmailee must be insecure enough to give in to emotional intimidation.

Loving couples are too caring to stoop this low.

Forgiveness Is Considered Unmanly

In our social network we treat the holding of a grudge as a strength. Sort of a "He called my herd of cows ugly and I'm going to get him for that." Everyone is so pleased when our hero rides over to his neighbor's spread and calls his sheep "oatmeal face" or something equally disgusting.

Women are often cast in the role of those who should forgive and "go along." Men frequently assume the title of avenger. They are supposed to set things right by getting even. These stereotypes are deadly when applied to a marriage relationship.

By accepting the insensitive role of avenger, we husbands pass on a highly destructive concept to our male children. They in turn tend to continue the cycle, producing generations of men who see the holding of a grudge as a manly art.

Naturally, women are also capable of withholding forgiveness, but our culture seems to hone vengefulness among men.

Jesus Christ enters our lives with a refreshing sense of relief. He gives us a spiritual outlook on forgiveness:

1. Christ gives us permission to forgive (Luke 11:4).

2. Christ gives us the example of forgiveness (Colossians 3:13).

3. Christ gives us the instruction to forgive (Matthew 18:21,22).

4. Christ gives us the motivation to forgive (Luke 6:37).

Results of Holding Grudges

When we refuse to forgive, we place terrible burdens on ourselves and our relationships. Some of those weights are:

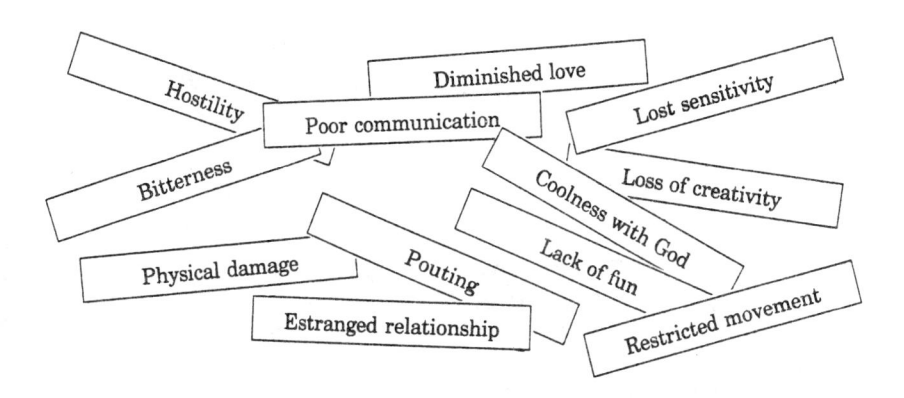

- Hostility
- Diminished love
- Lost sensitivity
- Poor communication
- Bitterness
- Coolness with God
- Loss of creativity
- Physical damage
- Pouting
- Lack of fun
- Estranged relationship
- Restricted movement

Herodias is said to have nursed a grudge against John the Baptist. The inability to deal with the problem resulted in the sudden demise of the prophet (Mark 6:19). Grudges also lob the head off marriages.

The Heavy Work Load of Unforgiveness

Holding a grudge should never be recommended for busy people. It takes far too much work to keep anger and bitterness alive. When we refuse to forgive, we must:

1. Keep track of why we are angry.

2. Remember to avoid the same mistake we accuse our partner of committing.

3. Periodically remind the individual that we have not forgotten the alleged offense.

4. Occasionally remind God that we are justified in our lack of forgiveness.

5. Avoid a feeling of freedom lest we forget what is supposed to be bugging us.

No small feat! Many of us will have to stay up late and get up early if we are to get all of our grudge-holding in.

Keep a Clean Slate

If we keep an account of every offense which our partner allegedly commits, we will soon have a list too cumbersome to carry. The Bible tells us that genuine love refuses to keep a tally.

> **First Corinthians 13:5 says, "Love keeps no record of wrongs."**

As a symbol each of us could take a piece of blank paper and write at the top "Past Offenses." In the middle of the page we could write "Forgiven and Forgotten." With deep sincerity we could then hand the paper to the partner we promised to love forever.

A lady from Phoenix said her husband had an affair nearly twenty years ago. For two decades Sally lived with the anger and suspicion which accompanied her memories.

"Joe's little escapade was in the back of my mind almost every day. I wondered who he was talking to, what he might be planning, what Joe would do when he was on a trip. I never found any evidence that he was having an affair, but my imagination would pick up little clues.

"No matter what we did or where we went, it was there. Finally a friend enlightened me. I was letting one mess-up ruin our relationship. The power of that one failure was still strangling our love for each other.

"Finally, I went to Joe and said, 'It's over. The bitterness I've had over you and Bonnie, it's gone.' And I started to cry.

"That's how I felt when Christ forgave me of my sins. I owed that same freedom to Joe and our relationship."

The Energy of Forgiveness

When we are weakened emotionally, partners tend to drag through the motions of a relationship without sparkle or spunk. The feeling of unfinished business and the drain of unresolved conflict sap our strength and take the life out of our marriage.

Notice the immediate relief when you tell your spouse you forgive him. Watch the change on his face. Sense the release of energy you feel in your own body.

Forgiveness gives a new vitality which was long lost under the pressure of grudge holding.

Couples that last have learned to let bygones be bygones.

Flexercise

1. Can you think of something Christ has forgiven you for?

2. Is there some event which has a stranglehold on your marriage relationship? Can you explain?

3. Are you holding a grudge as a security blanket? Explain.

4. Have you ever used a grudge as blackmail? Do you still hold that grudge?

The church and its members provide married couples with resources found nowhere else.

18

Christian Support

The early church probably never used the phrase *support group*. They had another term: *fellowship*.

Frequently, the first Christians lost their jobs, were hounded by authorities and were cast off by their family members. Before long, a large number gave their very lives for their newfound faith in Jesus Christ.

Their concept of fellowship went far beyond coffee after the morning service. Their fellow Christians gave them food, clothing, housing and prayer (Acts 2:42-47). Christians tried to bear each other's burdens.

The results from our interview say that the church is a significant "support group" for a large number of families. Many found strength from several levels. The church's structure and classes and its members had contributed measurably to making solid marriages.

Of course, that was not true for everyone; we are willing to admit that. Some local churches add nothing to the fiber of marriage. A few are even harmful to families. But we must conclude that churches and Christians on the whole have been a stabilizing force in many healthy marriages.

How does the church help?

Provides Biblical Teaching on Marriage

There is a cry for more information on how to build solid marriage and family relationships. Consequently, more is being said from the pulpit, the Sunday school class and in Bible studies. Seminars on marriage are being conducted in churches across the country.

Usually such seminars are well attended by a society hungry for help, and they have become excellent avenues for evangelism and outreach. It isn't uncommon to meet couples who became Christians while they sought counseling during marital difficulties. Ministers who help struggling couples can supply structure and guidelines to the faulty relationship. Couples do not forget the impact that type of help gives them.

Provides Form and Consistency

Regular church attendance creates a dependable routine when other things might be unstable. Many couples know they can go Sunday morning, participate in worship and listen to an optimistic message about a God who loves them. When everything seems to be falling apart, the church offers an anchor.

However, that does not work for everyone. If a marriage is rattling at its foundations, a meaningless, empty service will only add to the couples' feelings of futility. The service and message must connect with personal meaning in order to be effective.

Provides Release

There are two extremes in churches. On the one extreme, a church can be negative and make us feel bad. On the other, a church can be releasing and lift our burdens.

In the negative church, a parishioner believes he or she is rotten and the service confirms that ugly fact. The worshipper is helped only in that his bad feelings are confirmed. The message is, "You are correct about yourself:

You are useless, dumb and inept." Some people want exactly that affirmation because at least it removes their ambivalence. They thought they were useless and now it's been confirmed they are useless.

The second type of church puts an emphasis on forgiveness, potential, freedom, release and behavior adjustment. This church believes in a God who is involved in altering our daily lives for the better. Couples who attend this type of church may be more prone to an open, releasing relationship at home.

Churches which place a wholesome emphasis on confession are also a valued commodity. Often couples are consumed by their feelings of anger and revenge. Others are emotionally crippled because of mistakes, errors and sins they committed against loved ones. The opportunity to release these feelings in the presence of God can free a person to rebuild relationships at home.

"Before I became a Christian," Tanya explained, "I had a miserable attitude toward my parents and my spouse. The forgiveness I found in Jesus Christ allowed me to give most of that up. The rest of it I'm whittling away at."

Provides Help With Our Families

Young people often bolt from the church as soon as they can get away from home. This form of rebellion has a lot to do with establishing identity. Often they will go back to church to get married but they still keep a reasonable distance—until they have children. The arrival of children indicates an official "family" and that new stage sends people back to church in earnest.

The church which shows a genuine concern for children has an opportunity to minister to the entire family. If the church adds a fellowship for young couples to their children's ministry, they are on the road to helping couples for years to come.

People Are at the Center

A church is of maximum benefit to couples if individuals are allowed to make significant people connections. Couples need peers—other couples who are close in age and share many similarities in their marriages. Topics like arguing, diapers, formulas and communication are of particular interest to young married couples and they like to share their frustrations and insights with others who understand what they are going through.

Young couples also appreciate older married couples who give good, encouraging examples. What they don't enjoy is people who lean on them and tell them how to run their lives.

The Bible expects the older men and older women to provide helpful teaching to the younger men and women in the area of family living (Titus 2:1-5). When that information is transmitted in a correct spirit, young couples gobble it up.

"I felt a lot better when Cathy told me she thought about leaving her husband," Mary said. "Until then I wondered if I was evil or something. But Cathy told me how she and Ken worked it out and now they have been married for nearly twenty years. If no one shares with you, you start to think you are the only one who thinks that way."

Christian Literature

We tend to see our lives as harried in a fast changing society. Anything that can help us gain our bearings and level us off is eagerly accepted. Countless couples, including ourselves, have been able to shore up relationships because of literature that's been collected and read.

Something to be aware of: We don't need to study our marriages to death. Some of us suffer from *relationship fatigue*. We've been to countless seminars, read dozens of books and even rented a video or two. We've analyzed our marriage to the point where we have it down to a science. We carefully weigh the first words we say in the morning;

we leave a love note in his sneakers; we give him space; we even call our overdue mortgage payments "lagging opportunities." We believe there is an answer for every argument, poor habit and inconsideration in our relationship.

And there isn't.

But books do help. They have, in fact, saved marriages. Every couple could use one to tune up their relationship. They just don't need a dozen to add to their confusion.

Not the Same as Faith

Church attendance and a personal relationship with Jesus Christ are in different dimensions. Sitting in a church service and having faith in God are not the same (see the chapter, "Their Faith in God"). But the church, as an institution, can offer couples everywhere a tremendous amount of help. Pat and I, along with many other happily married couples, are grateful for the church and all it does to strengthen marriages.

Flexercise

1. How does your church help your marriage?
2. What would you like to see your church do further to help marriages?
3. Can you remember a time when Christians have helped your marriage when it was sagging?
4. What book on marriage would you recommend to others?
5. Which Christian couple do you see as a special encouragement to you? Why?

Perhaps if we really knew how God felt about sex, we'd be less hesitant to approach the subject.

19

Confusion in the Bedroom

We were having coffee when I flipped out my trusty 3 x 5 card and handed it to my unsuspecting friend. Smoothly I asked him to write three or four reasons why his magnificent marriage had lasted so many years.

Without hesitation he jotted down a few thoughts and returned the card. Smack in the middle of the list was the phrase, "Because of great sex."

I was really impressed. Not many men will tell you they have a good sex life. If they mention it at all, they often complain or gloss the subject over with jokes. This was refreshing and upbeat.

Months later I was in the church this man attends and I asked the congregation to list the reasons their marriages had lasted. When I later saw my friend, I told him, "I looked over the cards and no one wrote down 'Because of great sex.' What happened?"

"Well," he answered, "you don't pass that kind of answer down the aisle."

Because "You don't pass that kind of answer down the aisle," the interviews I conducted tell us almost nothing concerning our attitudes about sex. A few brave souls put down sex as one of their reasons for a great marriage, but they were not the norm. However, when I asked couples to list the three things they were most likely to argue over, the subject of sex was frequently listed.

What might we conclude from the relative silence? Let's guess. Either,

- ☐ We are not comfortable bringing up the subject.
- ☐ We are not comfortable discussing sex in a Christian setting.
- ☐ Sex is not a priority in marriage—especially after the first few years.
- ☐ We feel guilty and confused over sex.
- ☐ Sex is such a serious problem that few of us dare discuss it.
- ☐ A mixture of all the above reasons.
- ☐ None of the above reasons. We don't know what in the world is going on.

This is not to say that our interviews didn't tell us anything. A couple of things seemed evident from the people we talked to.

1. The respondents were definitely uncomfortable talking about sex.

In practically every group I spoke to, the subject of sex turned the room into a morgue. Members of the group listened hard, but their tongues became stone. When I asked if they would attend a seminar in a church discussing sex, not one person said he would show up. Even if they were willing to listen to someone discuss sex, they had no interest in discussing it themselves.

That surprised me in what is supposed to be an age of sexual openness.

2. The respondents were more willing to express negative feelings about sex than positive feelings.

One of two things is happening here. Either people have more negative feelings about sex than positive ones or they feel more comfortable expressing negative feelings.

Did you get all that?

A number of factors can contribute to creating negative feelings toward sex, including:

guilt feelings	confusion over facts
high utility bills	poor physical condition
hostility toward partner	general stress
disruptive children	lack of safe place
lack of imagination	feeling of inadequacy
feeling of divine disapproval	

Unfortunately, people who refuse to discuss the subject are unlikely to resolve their conflicts and get to the bottom of their feelings.

"I went to a one-day seminar on sex," said a banker from Iowa, "and I learned one thing which revolutionized our sex life. I didn't want to attend the seminar but I'm glad I did." We can learn to feel better about our sex life if we are willing to be educated.

The Sex Circle

To simplify the process of uncovering the roots of our negative attitudes toward sex, we have developed a "sex circle." If we have trouble with our sex life, our difficulty almost has to come from some combination of these four areas. Briefly, each section of the circle means this:

Physical. One or both partners are too tired, too overweight or too sick to regularly participate in sex. The solution is to keep ourselves in reasonably good condition.

Emotional. Factors like stress, hostility, lack of love, guilt, fear, anger, envy and other unresolved feelings diminish the possibility of a satisfying sex life.

Educational. In an era of supposed enlightenment, sexual ignorance is rampant. We know embarrassingly little about our partner's body, his turn-on procedures and even birth control. The problem is compounded by the attitude that we should not have to *learn* these things. We assume people just *know* these things.

Spiritual. A feeling persists that God allows sex but if the truth were known, He thinks it is a dirty little business—especially if we are enjoying it.

There is, in fact, only one biblical rule for sex between a married couple: Lock the door (Hebrews 13:4).

Positive Attitudes Toward Sex

The Bible cultivates healthy attitudes toward sex. Far from just allowing sexual activities, the Scriptures *absolutely insist on it.*

In 1 Corinthians 7:2-9 Paul outlines a number of reasons why we should maintain a positive sex life.

Reasons for Cultivating Good Sex

1. Sex is a natural need (verse 2).

2. Sex is the dues married couples pay (verse 3).

3. My mate owns my body, both men and women (verse 4).

4. We cannot separate except by mutual consent (verse 5).

5. Satan will use a poor sex life to kick you in the head (verse 6).

6. Celibacy is a gift which few have (verses 8,9).

Confusion in the Bedroom

Positive statements about sex are not limited to this passage. The Bible demonstrates an open, supportive attitude toward physical love. The freedom given to married couples may astound many of us.

Biblical Attitudes Toward Sex

1. God originated sex (Genesis 1:27,28).
2. Sex is a necessary good (1 Corinthians 7:5).
3. The first goal of sex is to please your partner (1 Corinthians 7:4).
4. There is absolute liberty for a married couple (Hebrews 13:4).
5. Sex should be satisfying (Proverbs 5:15-19).
6. Sex should be discussed and taught to our children within propriety (Check out the abundant number of scriptural references which are listed above.)

Yet in spite of the Bible's clear stand on the subject and the bombardment of sex on television, movies, videos, books and magazines, ignorance on the subject abounds. Interviews with teenagers demonstrate a lack of accurate information. And several myths still seem to persist among married couples even today. Let's list just a few samples.

Myths About Sex

Myth 1. Sex is a necessary evil.
Myth 2. Women have little interest in sex.
Myth 3. Masturbation causes physical or mental damage.
Myth 4. Contraceptives are un-Christian.
Myth 5. Men are great lovers.
Myth 6. Menopause erases a woman's desire for sex.
Myth 7. Hysterectomy removes ability for sex.
Myth 8. Older men and women do not have sex.
Myth 9. Wives should not take the initiative.

Myth 10. Too much sex will rot your brain.

Did you catch yourself believing one of these?

> **A man discussing sex once said: "The silence of the church only adds to the guilt and confusion."**

If married couples want more instruction about sex from a Christian perspective, they need to make it known. They can begin by telling their church leadership that they would appreciate a class or seminar which is practical and straightforward on this intimate but important subject.

Do yourself and your loved one a favor and become knowledgeable about sex. Couples that last are not afraid to take advantage of this special act.

Flexercise

1. Are your general feelings about sex positive or negative? Explain.

2. What do you feel interferes with you and your spouse having a more satisfying sex life?

3. When did you last discuss sex with other Christians? Was it helpful?

4. If your church arranged for a class discussing sex for married couples, would you attend? What form would you like to see that class take?

5. Look at the "Sex Circle." Which of the four areas would you like more help with?

6. How would you describe the biblical attitude toward marital sex? Does it surprise you?

What the two of you find interesting to do together is what counts.

20

Similar Interests

*E*ileen and Norm have been married for fourteen years. They each sent a note responding to our interview questions, and their answers rang with happiness. A key to their longevity was their pleasure over the same interests.

Norm said: "Our interests are amazingly similar. For example, our record collections were almost identical (classical)."

Eileen wrote: "We had a great many similar interests—music, books, etc."

Eileen and Norm are typical of many couples who married for more than just pure passion. Men and women are frequently blinded by their glands and marry strictly on the basis of physical drive. Couples that tend to last know they have similar interests before they exchange rings and are careful to develop new interests as their relationship matures.

John from Omaha struck the same chord, expanding his feelings to attitudes: "We share many similar attitudes (finances, government, education) and interests (music, children)."

As Doug explained: "We take an interest in each other's interests."

This is a tremendous improvement over the "desert" concept of marriage where couples see their relationship as merely a fight for survival. They drag themselves to work, struggle to corral the children, keep their house patched up and live for an evening when they can escape each other and get away to pursue their own interests.

Vibrant couples learn to develop shared activities which give more meaning to life than the bare necessities.

To help understand shared interests, let us loosely divide them into four general categories:

1. Quality interests
2. Goal-centered interests
3. Diversion interests
4. Spiritual interests

> "Each of you should look not only to your own interests, but also to the interests of others" (Philippians 2:4).

Quality Interests

Let's begin with the most satisfying. Quality interests are the activities which give both of us a deep feeling of personal worth. They say it is important to be doing something with you. "With you" is the significant phrase.

These interests must be warm and close. They will be more intimate in nature. Dinner, a picnic, skipping stones across a pond, holding hands at a concert, listening to dreams—each can amount to quality time.

The message conveyed is that *you* are more important to me than the activity. The activity is merely the vehicle which allows us to get closer and show our appreciation for each other. You can eat dinner at home for less money and possibly get a better meal, but that's not the point. The point is the two of you are together.

Some interests *massage the soul*. In many cases, women seem to appreciate these rituals more than men. This could be because men often fail to understand the need to strengthen the spirit.

These *enrichment activities* will cause each partner to feel like a better person for taking the time to cultivate this interest.

Goal-centered Interests

The label on these activities says, "We have to get this done." They are pointed, necessary and demanding. Hanging wallpaper falls into this category. It has to be done. Fixing toilets qualifies. Repairing the broken latch fits here.

As mundane as these tasks are, they are not unrelated to the soul. If they are not accomplished by ourselves or by professionals, their neglect begins to tear at our relationship and erode our sense of well-being.

> **Patty said, "Marriage will last if you don't remodel."**

A few couples actually see their relationship prosper through goal-related tasks, but more frequently the tasks are simply necessary and should be accomplished with the best attitude possible.

Diversion Interests

"We go to the stock car races on Saturday nights," Nadine told me in a dull tone. "Brian likes them and I go along to be along."

Hobbies, sports, shows and trips can be valuable but they are the most helpful if:

1. Both of you enjoy it.

2. It provides interaction between the two of you.

3. Neither partner feels like a third wheel.

4. Both mates can participate.

5. Each person fully understands why he is there.

When *none* of these elements are present, your partner might be better off going alone or with someone else who can more fully appreciate the fine art of toothpick collecting or whatever.

Diversion interests *cannot, must not, dare not* have a belittling effect on our partner. At that point, the activity is worse than no contact at all.

"I never mind going with her to antique shows," Kurt admitted. "She won't go alone and I realize what a big kick she gets out of it."

Does that sound like a good interest or a belittling one? Sounds great to me. The husband knows he fulfills a purpose. She needs a companion. He carries out an act of love. You can't beat that.

Spiritual Interests

Many of our respondents spoke in glowing terms of the spiritual interests they shared. They attended church together, worked in missionary endeavors, helped young people, sold Christian books, read the Bible and prayed.

Couples recognized the connection between Jesus Christ, the Holy Spirit and their relationship. They found great fulfillment pursuing those spiritual interests together. Those who were unable to share with their partner at some level on a spiritual dimension frequently expressed severe frustration.

Religious Addiction

A few couples have used their spiritual interests to hide from any personal or quality interests. They stay busy "working for the Lord" so they can avoid facing each other. In these cases, the "spiritual" becomes a cop-out which allows a shallow relationship to starve nearly to death.

Consider this possibility. When a husband or wife "serves Christ" constantly, without regard for his or her family, that person could simply be addicted to religion. They chase religious pursuits even though they knowingly desert the family which God expects them to emotionally support.

That person needs to recheck his or her spirituality.

A few Christians may have been directed to abandon their families to serve Christ. But only a few.

Take the Face Test

One way to evaluate your similar interests is to look at the following pictures and ask which ones most nearly fit your activity.

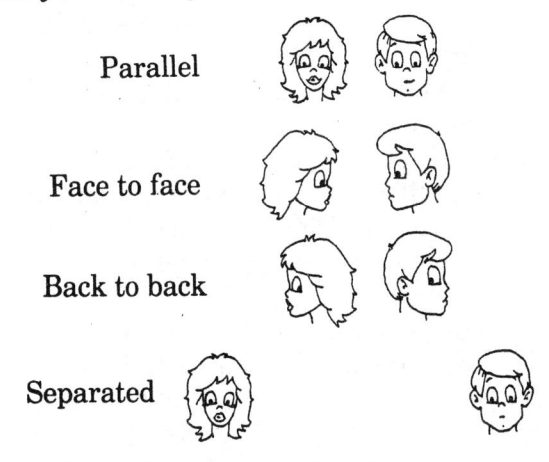

Parallel

Face to face

Back to back

Separated

If you go bowling, which of the four pictures will best describe your relationship during that activity?

If you go out to dinner, which of the four pictures will best describe your relationship during that activity?

If you go to a concert?
If you go hunting?
If you go skating?
If you go to a movie?
If you watch television?
If you go swimming?
If you go to Bible study?

Consider the interests you share. Do they help bind you together or are they part of the reason you drift apart?

Mere activity is not necessarily an indication of togetherness. Many activities do little to develop your relationship.

How do your activities measure up?

Who Controls Our Interests?

In order for shared interests to be helpful, they must be perceived as being mutual. Few things are as aggravating as the feeling that one person always gets his or her way. Similar interests cannot mean one person always buckles under to the other person.

Who died and made us King or Queen of Activities? Less mature people have a need for a relationship to revolve around them and them alone. Marriage is not a solar system and we are not the sun.

"Chris is never happy unless he is doing his own thing," Bev explained. "If it isn't fun for him, he can't imagine why we should do it. He gets bored in a minute and he lets you know it. If I think he won't enjoy it, I try not to even bring it up."

Like many husbands, Chris wants to operate from a place of power. He has little concept of equality. Because he is the man, Chris believes Bev should give in. If we scratched below his surface, we would probably discover that Chris feels it is particularly hard to be a man and he feels he should be pampered to compensate for the unusual pressure he faces. Naturally if we used the word *pampered,* he would become terribly indignant.

A marriage relationship is acutely handicapped if it is not thoroughly collegial. If either partner considers the other as less than equal, their hope for developing similar interests is painfully restricted. Our interests must move toward mutuality.

Developing New Interests

We do well to inherit the interests of our spouse. There must be hundreds of women who took up skeet shooting for their husbands and today love the sound of a spring release. Possibly he took up surfing for her. Nothing wrong with that.

Yet, there is a fascinating footnote here. There are surveys which suggest that happy couples receive the most fulfillment from similar interests which they found and nurtured together.

Neither of them scuba dived until they were married for four years. Today they are thrilled as catfish, finning their way across the bottom of pond after pond.

There must be several advantages to beginning new adventures together. Let's think out a few:

1. They reduce a parental attitude. (You are both fledglings.)

2. Each can share the excitement of new discoveries.

3. Your partner is less likely to ridicule your mistakes.

4. Each is humbled by his awkwardness.

5. Both have stories to tell of dropped bowling balls or birdies on #4 green.

You can probably add more reasons why discovering new interests might be better than only adopting your mate's. Certainly the freshness of experimenting contributes significantly to the joy, playfulness and sense of accomplishment we share.

Don't Have to Share Everything

We do not have to be interested in everything together. My wife has my blessing to go sky diving alone. If she wants to hunt mountain lions, I volunteer to protect the cabin while she's gone.

The more important question is: Do we have a core of interests which we like to pursue? Those select interests should be a huge help in keeping our marriage spirited.

Look at the "Circle of Interests" and see where most of your attention lies:

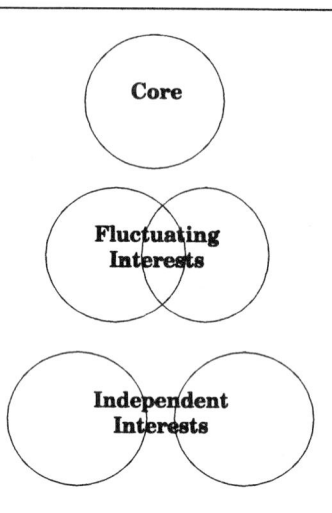

Independent interests means we do them without our spouse. We may do them alone or with other friends, but our partner is almost never involved.

Fluctuating interests. Our partner floats in and out. Occasionally he or she participates but not constantly.

Core interests. You and your partner hold a mutual passion for this activity or experience. You race each other for the door so you can get started. Smart couples build up at least a handful of these.

Where are most of my energies spent? Do I devote 90 percent of my time to the outer circle? Have I collected a good mix of all three?

Couples that last never underestimate the importance of shared interests.

Flexercise

1. How many interests do you have that you and your spouse are operating face to face?

2. What new interest are the two of you in the process of pursuing?

Similar Interests

3. How many of your interests are in the outer ring, middle ring and core ring?
4. What is one "quality" interest which you enjoy?

Understanding represents an investment. It does not come pre-packaged. It cannot be microwaved.

21

An Understanding Heart

I'm sorry we had to leave the restaurant early," Ben told his friend John, "but my wife was uncomfortable in there."

"Karen, uncomfortable?" John was startled. "You could have fooled me. I thought she was enjoying herself."

"No," Ben answered, "I could tell the place was really getting to her."

Ben saw something in Karen which John couldn't find. But Ben had an advantage which no detective would have. He had been married to her for six years and he *understood*.

Was it Karen's eyebrows? Maybe the clue was in the movement of her bottom lip. Was the evidence in what she had ordered from the menu or what she didn't order? Possibly Ben knew something about the scare Karen received in the fifth grade. Whatever it was, Ben *understood*.

We can be sure that Ben did not understand the evidence on their first date. He didn't know about it on the honeymoon. Nor did he quite comprehend the problem when they cut their first anniversary cake. Most likely it took years for him to discern what the difficulty was and how he could interpret that look or motion.

That is one of the advantages of a long-term marriage. We cultivate a friend who understands us. Short-term marriages seldom grow to that place of intimacy.

"There are two things I never kid about," said a seasoned husband. "I never joke about her bust size and I never make fun of her cooking. I learned that the hard way. You can tease her about sports, games, singing, almost anything; but you tread on those two areas at the risk of life and limb."

He probably didn't find that out during the first two weeks, but he found out eventually. And he left those subjects alone.

What Is Understanding?

When someone says, "I have an understanding husband," you can see the pride and joy in her face. She seems to realize what a rich treasure she has.

Understanding does not suggest pity or even tolerance, as valuable as that is. Rather understanding means:

A. I see what is going on in your life.
B. I know why you are that way.
C. I love you with your strengths and weaknesses.

Only a caring person is willing to fathom our moods, behaviors and idiosyncrasies. Only a loving person wants to know what makes us the complex people we are. Surface, superficial acquaintances lack the persistency it takes to get to know us.

If we have someone in our life who is willing to plumb the depths of our soul, we should thank God daily for that person.

Look at the high premium the Bible puts on understanding:

> Get wisdom, get understanding; do not forget my words or swerve from them. Do not forsake wisdom, and she will protect you; love her, and she will watch over you. Wisdom is supreme; therefore get wisdom. Though it cost all you have, get understanding (Proverbs 4:5-7).

> **Married partner: Though it cost you all you have, get understanding.**

When a husband does not like to come home evenings, some wives yell and hope to startle him into changing. Other wives attempt to understand why he is avoiding his family and see how they can help him come to grips with the dilemma. If you have been married for a while and taken time to understand your spouse, you probably have a fair idea of what he is running away from.

Understanding represents an investment. It does not come pre-packaged. It cannot be microwaved in three minutes.

Knowledge and Feelings

Like any other friendship, an effective marriage takes time. Only as months grow into years are we able to see the depths, shades, corners and crevices of our spouse. It takes a while for us to see how our mate acts and reacts. (That's knowledge.) Much more time is needed to comprehend *why* they are acting and reacting. (That's feelings.)

When we are able to put knowledge and feelings together, we have begun to reach understanding.

Casual acquaintances know you don't like to borrow money. Intimate friends may begin to understand why.

A married couple was piddling around at a park as their children played on the equipment. Mark and Diane were fifty feet apart when two men walking by asked Diane for directions. Crisply she pointed east, pivoted and hurried away from them.

"You really treated the men roughly," Mark commented as Diane returned to the picnic table. He had seen the action and gained some knowledge.

"I don't trust men in parks," she answered curtly.

Later, at home, Mark gave his wife the opportunity to open up and explain her behavior. Diane told him a sad story of her bad experience in a park as a child.

Mark then had the two ingredients necessary to understanding. He knew what she did and how she felt about it. The more transactions completed on this double level, the greater their potential is to become one.

Jesus Christ told us we hear a great deal of information and never understand what it means (Mark 4:12). Watching our mate's lifestyle will never be enough – our neighbors can do that. Intimate couples reach into the second layer and find out why.

My wife, Pat, likes to go to bed early. She always has and, frankly, I thought it was more than a little rude. Over the years we have occasionally had a bit of friction because of her nesting habits.

I knew what Pat did. I had knowledge. She parked it around 10:30 and that was the way it was.

One evening, like a revelation, it occurred to me. It would be unreasonable of Pat to expect me to go to bed at 10:30 and stay there. I would be screaming out, feeling like I was in prison. The confinement would be unbearable.

Then it dawned on me – that's how Pat feels. Her entire system screams out at the pressure of staying up late just as mine revulses at the thought of going to bed early.

Finally I began to understand. And understanding caused the resentment to disappear. Pat must be Pat just as Bill must be Bill.

The Time Element

But you object. You are a good student of humanity. You know what makes people tick. It won't take long for you to decipher your mate's feelings. You possess a special key that will unlock your partner's inner self.

You are a dangerous person!

There may be ways to gain insight into your partner and some special skills to make it easier, but there are no quick fixes. By its very nature, understanding comes only to those who are willing to put in the time.

The Bible speaks to the point: "A patient man has great understanding" (Proverbs 14:29).

Isn't the opposite true? An impatient man is a real bonehead.

When we first get married, there are some things most of us don't understand. See if any of these ring a bell.

Men have trouble understanding:

Why women cry.

Why they want to be held.

Why it takes one hour for them to get ready.

Why they don't like to go out on the spur of the moment.

Why they don't like jokes about their bodies.

Why foreplay is important.

Why listening is vital.

Why women dress for other women.

Women have trouble understanding:

Why men watch football games when the outcome is not in doubt.

Why they can't leave the remote control alone.

Why they have a breast fixation.

Why they crawl on their bellies in the mud to hunt ducks.

Why they don't like women bosses.

Why they don't share feelings.

Why they don't need foreplay.

Why they can't find the children's pajamas.

These are merely the beginning. Who is there to understand why we are afraid of being abandoned or why we don't want to raise teenagers? Who will listen to our feelings about alcohol, sex, faith or motherhood? Patient, available marriage partners gain insight as their relationship matures.

Fortunately, understanding is not dependent on our experiences. Understanding requires that we try to get in touch with our partner's experiences.

The apostle Paul prayed that the Christians at Philippi would see their love grow, particularly in two areas: in knowledge and in depth of insight (1:9). It is reasonable to pray for a greater sensitivity to what our spouse feels. As we better comprehend what goes on inside that person, we make constructive change a greater possibility.

What are the important pillars which will we hold understanding?

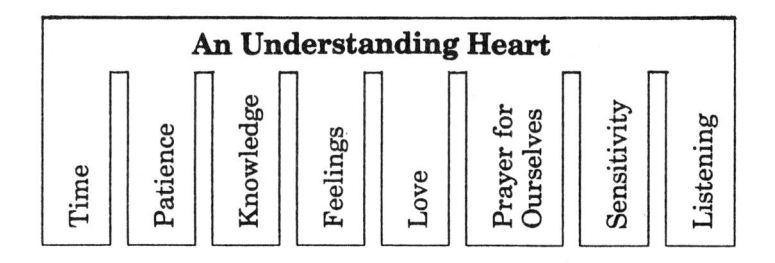

An Understanding Heart

| Time | Patience | Knowledge | Feelings | Love | Prayer for Ourselves | Sensitivity | Listening |

None of these pillars are male or female. Everyone is capable of an understanding heart if he is willing to work at it.

If a husband is the adult-child of an alcoholic, he probably suffers from serious repercussions. Most likely his wife does not come from a similar background and, consequently, she cannot feel what he feels. That isn't bad. Let's hope she never feels what he feels. But she can come to understand what he feels. That insight can help him heal.

Have you ever seen a person after he has shared a problem with another individual? Have you looked at his face when he said those transforming words, "He understood"?

Every marriage should be blessed with that phrase.

166   WHAT MAKES A MARRIAGE LAST?

Flexercise

1. Is there a way that you can tell when your mate is upset?

2. What have you grown to understand about your spouse?

3. Do you have midnight talks about your feelings? Have they proved helpful?

4. There are eight pillars under the illustration about an understanding heart. Which pillars are your strongest ones?

5. Which of those eight pillars do you wish your partner could show more of?

Just a Reminder

*M*arriage is one of the greatest joys in life. In hundreds of interviews we could see the happiness and the satisfaction jumping out. There were twinkles in their eyes, grins on their faces and even excitement in their voices. We read cards where the writers' enthusiasm caused them to blur their handwriting because they wrote with such energy.

It's a mistake to make marriage problem-centered. That's like having a beautiful flower garden and yet getting angry because you have to mow around it. Loving couples don't ignore the difficulties, but they do spend more time smelling the flowers.

The prize of a good marriage is within the reach of most of us. Merchants, bakers and candlestick makers all have the potential which God has given. Walk through this world together and drink deeply from a partnership which could be tremendously fulfilling.

Making Good Marriages Better

Quantity   **Total**

_____   **Managing Stress in Marriage** by Bill and Vonette Bright. A delightfully candid book with practical help for busy couples who experience added stress from the hectic pace of dual careers or ministry involvement. ISBN 0-89840-272-7/$7.95 $ _____

_____   **Building Your Mate's Self-Esteem** by Dennis and Barbara Rainey. Ten essential building blocks for strengthening your mate's self-esteem, with creative ideas for immediate results. ISBN 0-89840-105-4/$8.95 $ _____

_____   **Keeping Your Marriage From Burning Out** by William L. Coleman. Discover ways to refuel the flame in a lackluster or troubled marriage and prevent marital burnout. ISBN 0-89840-254-9/$7.95 $ _____

_____   **When Two Walk Together** by Richard and Mary Strauss. Join Richard and Mary Strauss in their discovery of intimacy through better communication. ISBN 0-89840-216-6/$7.95 $ _____

Your Christian bookseller should have these products in stock. Please check with him before using this "Shop by Mail" form.

Send completed order form to: **HERE'S LIFE PUBLISHERS, INC.**
P. O. Box 1576
San Bernardino, CA 92402-1576

Name _____
Address _____
City _____ State _____ Zip _____

☐ Payment enclosed
   (check or money order only)
☐ Visa   ☐ Mastercard
_____
Expiration Date _____
Signature _____

**For faster service, call toll free:
1-800-950-4457**

ORDER TOTAL $ _____

SHIPPING and HANDLING $ _____
($1.50 for one item, $0.50 for each additional. Do not exceed $4.00.)

APPLICABLE SALES TAX (CA 6.75%) $ _____

TOTAL DUE $ _____

Please allow 2 to 4 weeks for delivery.
Prices subject to change without notice.

WMM 274-3

Building Stronger Families

Quantity   **Total**

_____ **Pulling Weeds, Planting Seeds: Growing Character in Your Life and Family** by Dennis Rainey. An inspiring collection of pointed reflections on personal and family life with an abundance of practical insights for everyday living. ISBN 0-89840-217-4/hardcover, $12.95 $ _____

_____ **The Dad Difference: Creating an Environment for Your Child's Sexual Wholeness** by Josh McDowell and Dr. Norm Wakefield. Sets the stage for fathering that will dramatically improve parent/teen relationships. Practical examples of role modeling and father/children activities. ISBN 0-89840-252-2/$8.95 $ _____

_____ **Family Fitness Fun** by Charles Kuntzleman. Enjoy the sense of freedom that comes with feeling healthier and more energetic by tapping into this hassle-free handbook to a wholesome family lifestyle. A book for the entire family with more than 180 stimulating strategies and activities for both parents and children. ISBN 0-89840-279-4/$9.95 $ _____

Your Christian bookseller should have these products in stock. Please check with him before using this "Shop by Mail" form.

Send completed order form to: **HERE'S LIFE PUBLISHERS, INC.**
P. O. Box 1576
San Bernardino, CA 92402-1576

Name _____

Address _____

City _____ State _____ Zip _____

☐ Payment enclosed
   (check or money order only)
☐ Visa   ☐ Mastercard
_____

Expiration Date _____
Signature _____

**For faster service, call toll free:
1-800-950-4457**

ORDER TOTAL $ _____

SHIPPING and HANDLING $ _____
($1.50 for one item, $0.50 for each additional. Do not exceed $4.00.)

APPLICABLE SALES TAX (CA 6.75%) $ _____

TOTAL DUE $ _____

Please allow 2 to 4 weeks for delivery.
Prices subject to change without notice.